5

CANADIAN GRAMMAR SPECTRUM

REFERENCE AND PRACTICE

John Eastwood

OXFORD
UNIVERSITY PRESS

OXFORD
UNIVERSITY PRESS

Oxford University Press is a department of the University of Oxford.
It furthers the University's objective of excellence in research, scholarship, and education by publishing worldwide.
Oxford is a registered trade mark of Oxford University Press in the UK and in certain other countries.

Published in Canada by
Oxford University Press
8 Sampson Mews, Suite 204,
Don Mills, Ontario M3C 0H5 Canada

www.oupcanada.com

First Edition published in 2012

Oxford Practice Grammar: Intermediate was originally published in 2006. This edition is published by arrangement with Oxford University Press, Great Clarendon Street, Oxford OX2 6DP, United Kingdom.

Library and Archives Canada Cataloguing in Publication

Eastwood, John
Canadian grammar spectrum 5 : reference and practice / John Eastwood.

Includes index.
Previously published as part of: Eastwood, John. Oxford
practice grammar.
Intermediate, 2006.
ISBN 978-0-19-544834-4

1. English language—Grammar—Problems, exercises, etc.
2. English language—Textbooks for second language learners. I. Title.

PE1128.E26 2011 428.2'4 C2011-903940-0

Oxford University Press is committed to our environment.
This book is printed on Forest Stewardship Council® certified paper,
harvested from a responsible sources.

FSC
www.fsc.org
MIX
Paper from
responsible sources
FSC® C004071

Printed and bound in Canada.

1 2 3 4 — 15 14 13 12

Contents

Nouns and articles

This, my, some, a lot of, etc.

Pronouns

Adjectives and adverbs

Prepositions

Verbs with prepositions and adverbs

Reported speech

Relative clauses

Conditionals

Linking words

Review test

Appendices

Answer key

Index

Introduction

Canadian Grammar Spectrum is a series of books, each written at the appropriate level for you at each stage in your study of English. The series is intended for your use either in a classroom or when working independently on your own time.

The books are divided into two- to four-page units, each of which covers an important grammar topic. Each unit starts with an explanation of the grammar and this is followed by a set of practice exercises. A test at the end of each book gives the opportunity for more practice and enables you to assess how much you have learned. Answers to the exercises and the test are provided at the back of the book.

You may want to choose the order in which you study the grammar topics, perhaps going first to those giving you problems. (Topics are listed in the Contents page at the front of each book and in the Index at the back.) Alternatively, you may choose to start at the beginning of each book and work through to the end.

The emphasis throughout this book is on the meaning and use of the grammatical forms. The explanations of grammar are descriptions of how English works; they are a guide to help you understand, not rules to be memorized. It is often more effective to look at examples of English rather than to read statements about it, and the grammar explanations are supported by lots of examples of everyday conversational English.

Key to symbols

The symbol / (oblique stroke) between two words means that either word is possible. *I may/might go* means that *I may go* and *I might go* are both possible. In exercise questions this symbol is also used to separate words or phrases which are possible answers.

Parentheses ( ) around a word or phrase in the middle of a sentence mean that it can be left out. *There's (some) milk in the fridge* means that there are two possible sentences: *There's some milk in the fridge* and *There's milk in the fridge*.

The symbol ~ means that there is a change of speaker. In the example *How are you? ~ I'm fine, thanks*, the question and answer are spoken by different people.

The symbol ▶ in an exercise indicates that a sample answer is given.

Present Progressive or Simple Present?

1 Now or sometimes?

MILA VARGAS IS A TV REPORTER.

MILA IS ON GUY'S TALK SHOW.

PRESENT PROGRESSIVE

We use the Present Progressive for something happening now. *I am speaking to you live* means that Mila is in the middle of a live broadcast. Here are some more examples.

*It's **raining** right now.*
*I'm **watching** this show.*
*Look. That man **is taking** a photo of you.*

SIMPLE PRESENT

We use the Simple Present for repeated actions. *I often speak live to the camera* means that she does it again and again.

*It always **rains** on the weekend.*
*I **watch** television most weekends.*
*He's a photographer. He **takes** lots of photos.*

2 Thoughts, feelings, and states

We normally use the Simple Present to talk about thoughts and feelings.

*I **think** it's a good show.* *Mila **likes** her job.*

We also use it to talk about states and permanent facts.

*Reporting **means** a lot to her.* *Paper **burns** easily.*

We also use the Simple Present in **I promise, I agree, I refuse**, etc.

*I **promise** I'll write to you.* *It's all right. I **forgive** you.*

3 Temporary or permanent?

PRESENT PROGRESSIVE

We use the Present Progressive for a routine or situation that we see as temporary (for a short period).

*I'm **working** at a community centre for six weeks.*
*Right now they'**re living** in a very small apartment.*

SIMPLE PRESENT

We use the Simple Present for a routine or situation that we see as permanent.

*I **work** at a community centre. It's a permanent job. They **live** in a very nice apartment.*

4 Always

PRESENT PROGRESSIVE

We can use **always** with the Present Progressive to mean "very often," usually with the added meaning of "too often."

*Effem **is always inviting** friends here.*
(= He invites them very often.)
*I'**m always making** careless mistakes.*
(= I make careless mistakes too often.)

SIMPLE PRESENT

Always with the Simple Present means "every time."

*Effem **always invites** us for dinner on Sunday.*
(= He invites us every Sunday.)
*I **always make** careless mistakes on tests.*
(= I make mistakes on every test.)

Practice

A Present Progressive or Simple Present? (1–2)

At work, Martin is talking to Alain in the hallway. Complete their conversation. Write the Present Progressive or Simple Present form of the verbs.

Martin: (▶) Are you looking (you/look) for someone?
Alain: Yes, (▶) I need (I/need) to speak to Neil. He isn't in his office.
Martin: (1) .... (he/talk) to the boss right now.
(2) .... (I/think)
(3) .... (they/discuss) money.
Alain: Oh, right. And what about you? (4) .... (you/look) for someone, too?
Martin: Yes—Linda. (5) .... (you/know) where she is?
Alain: Oh, she isn't here today. She only (6) .... (work) four days a week.
(7) .... (she/not/work) on Fridays. She'll be here on Monday.
Martin: Thank you. (8) .... (you/know) a lot about Linda.
Alain: Well, most days (9) .... (I/give) her a ride, or
(10) .... (she/give) me one. (11) ....
(she/live) very close to me. (12) .... (it/save) gas.
Martin: Yes, (13) .... (I/agree). Good idea.
Well, (14) .... (I/waste) my time here then. I'll get back to my computer.

B Present Progressive or Simple Present? (1–3)

Complete the sentences. Write the Present Progressive or Simple Present form of the verbs.

▶ I'm writing (I/write) to my parents. I write (I/write) to them every weekend.

1 .... (it/snow) outside. .... (it/come) down pretty hard—look.

2 Normally .... (I/start) work at eight o'clock, but .... (I/start) at seven this week. We're very busy right now.

3 My car is in the garage, so .... (I/go) to work on the bus this week. Usually .... (I/drive) to work.

4 The sun .... (rise) in the east, remember. It's behind us so .... (we/travel) west.

5 I'm afraid I have no time to help you now. .... (I/write) a report. But .... (I/promise) I'll give you some help later.

6 .... (I/want) a new car. .... (I/save) up to buy one.

C Always (4)

Complete the sentences. Use *always* and the Present Progressive or Simple Present.

▶ Vivienne: Yuri talks too much, doesn't he?
Keisha: Yes, and he's always talking about hockey.

▶ Courtney: You forget your keys every time.
Marc: I try to remember them, but I always forget .

1 Cameron: Sarah takes the train every day, doesn't she?
Danilo: Yes, ... the train.

2 Patti: Janna misses lectures way too often, in my opinion.
Kerry: I agree. .... lectures.

3 Mike: Every time I drive along here, I go the wrong way.
Nicolette: But it's very simple, isn't it? Why .... the wrong way?

4 Dani: Jesse and Jeff argue too much, I think.
June: I know. ....

Past Progressive or Simple Past?

1 Introduction

A reporter is interviewing Gilbert and Ruby.

Reporter: *Gilbert and Ruby, tell me what you* ***saw****.*

Ruby: *Well, when we* ***were driving*** *home last night, we* ***saw*** *a strange object in the sky.*

Gilbert: *As we* ***were coming*** *down the hill into town, it just suddenly* ***appeared*** *in front of us. We* ***stopped*** *the car and* ***got*** *out.*

Ruby: *It* ***was*** *a very clear night. The stars* ***were twinkling****.*

Gilbert: *It* ***was*** *a spaceship. It* ***seemed*** *very big. It* ***had*** *some strange writing on the side. And a light* ***was flashing*** *on the top.*

Ruby: *As we* ***were watching*** *it, it suddenly* ***flew*** *away and* ***disappeared****.*

PAST PROGRESSIVE	SIMPLE PAST
We use the Past Progressive for an action that we were in the middle of. *We* ***were driving*** *home.* (We were in the middle of our trip.) *A light* ***was flashing****.* We do not normally use the Past Progressive for states. NOT ~~*The spaceship was seeming ...*~~ NOT ~~*It was having writing ...*~~ NOT ~~*I wasn't knowing ...*~~	We use the Simple Past for a complete action in the past. *We* ***drove*** *home.* (We finished our trip.) *The spaceship* ***flew*** *away.* We also use the Simple Past (not normally the Progressive) for states. *The spaceship* ***seemed*** *very big.* *It* ***had*** *writing on the side.* *I* ***didn't know*** *what it was.*

2 It happened as I was driving

We often use the Past Progressive and Simple Past together when one (shorter) action comes in the middle of another (longer) one.

As we ***were driving*** *down the hill, a strange object* ***appeared*** *in the sky.*
While Laura ***was sitting*** *in the yard, it suddenly* ***began*** *to rain.*
You ***drove*** *right past me when I* ***was waiting*** *for the bus.*

The appearance of the strange object comes in the middle of the longer action, the drive down the hill.

Longer action: *We were driving down the hill.*
Shorter action: *An object appeared.*

In the three sentences above, the Past Progressive comes after **as, while** or **when** (***As*** we ***were driving*** ...). We can also use **when** before the Simple Past.

We ***were driving*** *down the hill* ***when*** *a strange object* ***appeared*** *in the sky.*
Amed ***was making*** *lunch* ***when*** *the phone* ***rang****.*

But we use two Simple Past verbs for one action after another.

When we ***saw*** *the spaceship, we* ***stopped*** *the car.* (= We saw it and then we stopped.)

3 The sun was shining

PAST PROGRESSIVE	SIMPLE PAST
We often use the Past Progressive to describe the background. The sun **was shining.** The stars **were twinkling.**	We use the Simple Past for actions in a story. We **arrived** at the beach. The aliens **landed** quietly.

Practice

A Past Progressive or Simple Past? (1–2)

Jeff is always having accidents. His girlfriend Shannon is talking about some of the accidents. Write her sentences from these notes. Each sentence has one verb in the Past Progressive and one in the Simple Past.

▶ when/he/carry/a suitcase/he/drop/it/on his foot
When he was carrying a suitcase, he dropped it on his foot.

▶ he/break/his leg/when/he/ski
He broke his leg when he was skiing.

1 he/sit down/on a chair/while/I/paint/it

....

2 as/he/run/for a bus/he/collide/with a lamppost

....

3 his hair/catch/fire/when/he/fry/onion rings

....

4 when/he/hold/a beautiful vase/he/suddenly/drop/it

....

5 he/sit/in the backyard/when/a bee/sting/him/on the nose

....

B Past Progressive or Simple Past? (1–2)

Write the correct form of the verb.

Sandy: I hear the lights (▶) went (go) out in your building last night.

Kaya: Yes, (▶) I was watching (I/watch) a documentary on TV when suddenly (1) .... (we/lose) all power. But (2) .... (it/come) on again after about ten minutes.

Jenny: Jeanne (3) .... (come) down the stairs when the lights (4) .... (go) out. She almost (5) .... (fall) over.

Ricardo: Matthew and I (6) .... (play) cards at the time.

Joe: (7) .... (I/work) on the computer. (8) .... (I/lose) a whole hour's work. But this morning (9) .... (I/get) up early and (10) .... (do) it again.

C Past Progressive or Simple Past? (1–3)

Find the second part of each sentence. Write each verb in the correct form.

▶	Lian (have) a beautiful dream	when she (touch) the wire.
▶	When Georges (see) the question,	when I (find) a ten-dollar bill in it.
1	The train (wait)	~~when the alarm clock (ring).~~
2	I (read) a library book	the crowd (rush) in.
3	Arianna (get) an electric shock	~~he (know) the answer immediately.~~
4	When the doors (open),	they (see) that the sun (shine).
5	When the campers (wake),	when we (arrive) at the station.

▶ Lian was having a beautiful dream when the alarm clock rang.

▶ When Georges saw the question, he knew the answer immediately.

1 ....

2 ....

3 ....

4 ....

5 ....

Present Perfect or Simple Past? (1)

1 I have done or I did?

The Present Perfect tells us about the past and the present. The Rockets have won the cup, so it's theirs now.	The Simple Past tells us about the past, a time which is finished. Last year is in the past.

We use the Simple Past (not the Present Perfect) to talk about times in the past such as **yesterday, last week, in 1994, a hundred years ago.**

*We **watched** a game **last week**.* NOT ~~*We have watched a game last week.*~~
***Long ago** dinosaurs **lived** here.* NOT ~~*Long ago dinosaurs have lived here.*~~

Here are some more examples.

PRESENT PERFECT	SIMPLE PAST
*Faye **has packed** her suitcase.*	*Faye **packed** her suitcase **last night**.*
(So her things are in the suitcase now.)	(Her things may be unpacked now.)
*Manuel **has fixed** the chair.*	*Manuel **fixed** the chair.*
(So it's all right now.)	(It may be broken again now.)
*The plane **has** just **landed**.*	*The plane **landed ten minutes ago**.*
***I've turned** the heat on.* (It's on now.)	*I **turned** the heat on **earlier**, but it's off again now.*
***I've dropped** my calculator.* (It's on the floor now.)	*I **dropped** my calculator, but it seems to be OK.*

2 I've done it. I did it yesterday.

Komoko: *We**'ve bought** a new car.*
Tom: *Oh, have you? What kind?*
Komoko: *A Prius. We **bought** it last week.*

We often give a piece of news in the Present Perfect, e.g. *We've bought a new car.* (The car is ours now.) We use the Simple Past, e.g. *We bought it last week,* to give details or to ask for details about things such as when and where it happened.

Here are some more examples.

***I've found** my wallet. ~ Oh, good. Where **did** you **find** it?*
*Your package **has arrived**. The mail carrier **brought** it at eight o'clock.*
*They**'ve closed** the factory. ~ Really? When **did** they **do** that?*

3 Structures with **for, since,** and **last**

PRESENT PERFECT	SIMPLE PAST
We can say that something hasn't happened for a long time or since a specific time in the past.	We can say that it was a long time since something happened or when was the last time it happened.
*We **haven't had** a party **since** Halloween.*	*Halloween was **the last time** we **had** a party.*

Practice

A I have done or I did? (1)

Write the correct verb form.

▶ I've done.......... (I/do) all the housework. The apartment is really clean now.
▶ A young couple bought.......... (buy) the house next door. But they didn't live there long.
1 Our guests .... (arrive). They're sitting in the living room.
2 There's still a problem with the television. Someone .... (fix) it, but then it broke again.
3 .... (I/lose) my bank card. I can't find it anywhere.
4 The game .... (start). The Jets are playing well.
5 My dog .... (run) away from home. But she came back two days later.
6 Daniel .... (earn) some money last week. But he's already spent it all.
7 .... (we/plant) an apple tree in the yard. Unfortunately, it died.
8 Prices .... (go) up. Everything is more expensive this year.
9 Someone .... (turn) on the radio. What's that song called?
10 .... (I/call) the office at eleven to speak to the manager, but he isn't there today.
11 .... (I/make) a cake. Would you like a piece?
12 The runner Haile Gebrselassie .... (break) the world record for the marathon in 2007. Then one year later, he ran it in an even faster time.

B I've done it. I did it yesterday. (2)

Things that have happened today are on the radio and TV news.
Report the news using the Present Perfect and Simple Past.

▶ the prime minister/visit McGill University/speak to students there/earlier today
The prime minister has visited McGill University. He spoke to students there earlier today.....

1 the bus drivers/go on strike/stop work/at twelve o'clock

....

2 the Governor General/arrive in Toronto/fly there/in a helicopter

....

3 two men/escape from Kingston Penitentiary/get away/during the night

....

4 the author Yann Martel/write a new book/it come out/last week

....

5 Sharon Cherop/win the women's marathon/run it/in 2 hours 22 minutes

....

C Structures with **for**, **since**, and **last** (3)

Complete the conversations.

▶ Varun: This car is filthy. I haven't been to the car wash for about a year.
Sanjay: What! You mean it's been twelve months since you last went.......... to the car wash?
1 Laura: I haven't used my camera recently. June was the last time I took a photo.
Salma: Really? I'm surprised you .... June.
2 Gloria: I haven't seen Andrew for weeks.
Naeem: I haven't either. It's been .... him.
3 Kim: What about a game of cards? We haven't played since your birthday.
Eugenia: Really? You mean my birthday .... cards?
4 Isa: I feel terrible. It's been three days since I ate anything.
Anna: What did you say? You .... three days?

Present Perfect or Simple Past? (2)

1 I've been or I was?

PRESENT PERFECT

We use the Present Perfect for a state which has gone on up to the present. (David is still in the hospital.)

*We've **lived here** for ten years.*
(And we still live here.)

SIMPLE PAST

We use the Simple Past for a state in the past, in a period which is finished. (David's stay in the hospital is over.)

*We **lived there** for ten years.*
(We don't live there now.)

2 Have you (ever) ...? and Did you (ever) ...?

PRESENT PERFECT

We use the Present Perfect for actions in a period of time up to the present.

*This young director **has made** four movies so far.*

He has made movies means that it is possible he will make more movies.

Here are some more examples.

***Have** you **ever been** to Peru? ~ Yes, twice.*
***I've played** lacrosse before.*
***We've never had** any money.*

SIMPLE PAST

We use the Simple Past for actions in the past, a period which is finished.

*The director **made** many movies in his long career.*

He made movies means that his career in movies is over. He won't make any more.

*Did Mom **ever go** to Peru? ~ Yes, I think so.*
*I **played** lacrosse in college.*
*We **never had** any money in those days.*

3 Today, this week, etc.

PRESENT PERFECT

We use **today** and phrases with **this** for a period up to the present.

*It **hasn't snowed today**.*
***Have** you **seen this** week's magazine?*

SIMPLE PAST

We use **yesterday** and phrases with **last** for a past period.

*It **snowed yesterday**.*
***Did** you **see last** week's magazine?*

But sometimes **today** etc. can mean a past period. Compare:

*I **haven't seen** Hannah **today**.*
(It's still daytime.)
***Has** the mail **come this** morning?*
(It's still morning.)

*I **didn't see** Hannah at work **today**.*
(The working day is over.)
***Did** the mail **come this** morning?*
(It's later in the day.)

Practice

A I've been or I was? (1)

Complete this letter to a newspaper. Write the Present Perfect or Simple Past.

A few days ago I (▶) learned (learn) that someone plans to tear down the Grand Central Tavern. This bar (▶) has been (be) an important part of our town for decades. It (1) .... (stand) on Main Street for 50 years. It (2) .... (be) famous in the old days, and some of the old Maple Leafs (3) .... (drink) there, they say. I (4) .... (live) in Essex all my life. The locals (5) .... (know) about the plans for less than a week and already there's a "Save Our Bar" campaign. Last week we (6) .... (be) happy, but this week we're angry. We will stop them, you'll see.

B Have you (ever) ...? and Did you (ever) ...? (2)

Look at each conversation and choose the best sentence, a) or b).

▶ Have you heard about the woman walking across Canada? ~ Yes, she's reached the Rockies.
a) ☑ The walk is continuing. b) ☐ The walk has finished.

1 Have you ever played beach volleyball? ~ Yes, we played it on vacation.
a) ☐ The vacation is still going on. b) ☐ The vacation is over.

2 Did you know old Mr. Rajabi? ~ No, I never met him.
a) ☐ Mr. Rajabi is probably alive. b) ☐ Mr. Rajabi is probably dead.

3 Sean McInnis is a great curler. ~ Yes, he's helped the Canadian team win many games.
a) ☐ Sean McInnis still plays for the team. b) ☐ Sean McInnis has left the team.

C Today, this week, etc. (3)

Write *this*, *last*, *today*, or *yesterday*.

▶ Last ...... month prices went up, but this .... month they have fallen a little.

1 It's been dry so far .... week, but .... week was very wet.

2 I went shopping earlier .... and spent all the money I earned ....

3 We didn't have many visitors .... year. We've had a lot more .... year.

4 I don't feel so tired now. We got up very late .... morning. I felt really tired .... when we got up so early.

D Present Perfect or Simple Past? (Pages 6 and 8)

Write the verbs.

Noa: (▶) Have you heard ...... (you/hear) the news about David?
Holly: No. (1) .... (what/happen)?
Noa: (2) .... (he/have) an accident. He was walking down some stairs. (3) .... (he/fall) and (4) .... (break) his leg.
Holly: Oh, how awful! When (5) .... (it/happen)?
Noa: Yesterday afternoon. Melanie (6) .... (tell) me about it last night.
Holly: Last night! (7) .... (you/know) about it since last night, and (8) .... (you/not/tell) me!
Noa: Well, (9) .... (I/not/see) you last night. And (10) .... (I/not/see) you today, until now.
Holly: I hope he's all right. (11) .... (he/have) lots of accidents, you know. (12) .... (he/do) the same thing about two years ago.

Present Perfect or Present Perfect Progressive?

1 I have been doing or I have done?

*Yan **has been fixing** the car.*

We use the Present Perfect Progressive for an action happening over a period of time. We are thinking of Yan doing the job and getting oil on his hands.

*Yan **has fixed** the car.*

We use the Present Perfect or a complete action. We are thinking of the finished job and the result of the repair—that the car is all right now.

Here are some more examples.

OVER A PERIOD (**have been doing**)

*We**'ve been touring** the east coast.*
*A strong wind **has been blowing** all day.*
*Sophia is out of breath. She**'s been running**.*
***I've been writing** an essay. I'm tired now.*

We normally use the Present Perfect Progressive when we say <u>how long</u>.

*Ravenna **has been playing** music **all day**.*
***I've been ironing** shirts **since** ten o'clock.*
***How long have** you **been learning** to drive?*

COMPLETE (**have done**)

*We**'ve finished** our tour of the east coast.*
*The wind **has blown** a tree over.*
*Sophia is here at last. She**'s run** all the way.*
***I've written** an essay. I can hand it in now.*

We normally use the Present Perfect when we say <u>how much/many</u>.

*Ravenna **has played** at least **twenty** albums.*
***I've ironed eight** shirts.*
***How many** driving lessons **have** you **had**?*

2 States and actions

We cannot normally use the progressive form with a state verb.

***I've known** the secret for a long time.* NOT ~~*I've been knowing the secret.*~~
*My parents **have had** this car for about ten years.*
*We**'ve** never **been** very happy here, I'm afraid.*

Live and **work** (= have a job) can be Present Perfect or Present Perfect Progressive, with no difference in meaning.

*We**'ve been living** here since 2009.* OR *We**'ve lived** here since 2009.*
*Janna **has been working** for the company for three years now.* OR *Janna **has worked** for the company for three years now.*

Practice

A I have been doing or I have done? (1)

Read these conversations and write the correct form of the verb.
Use the Present Perfect or Present Perfect Progressive.

► Jen: I feel really tired.
Matt: It's because you've been doing........ (you/do) too much.
Sarah: Well, at least I've finished............... (I/finish) that report now, and I can relax.

1 Natalie: Someone .... (leave) the ladder outside—look.
Donald: I think that was Mike. .... (he/clean) the windows. I don't think .... (he/finish) yet.

2 Heidi: You've got mud on your shoes.
Gilbert: It's all right, I'll take them off. .... (I/work) in the garden.
Heidi: Yes, it looks a lot better. Well done. .... (you/do) a good job.

3 Edwin: .... (I/hear) that you and Ruby are building a garage. How long .... (you/do) that?
Andrew: Oh, for about a month now. ....(we/do) about half of it.

B I have been doing or I have done? (1)

What would you ask in these situations? Use the Present Perfect or Present Perfect Progressive.

► Your friend is wearing glasses. You've never seen him with glasses on before. Ask him how long ...
How long have you been wearing glasses?..

► Nick is playing video games. Ask him how many ...
How many video games have you played?..

1 You meet a group of people walking across the province. Ask them how many kilometres ...
....

2 A road crew is digging up the road outside Shauna's house. Ask her how long ...
....

3 Adelinda is taking lots of photos of you and your friends. Ask her how many ...
....

4 You have just woken up from an afternoon nap and you see that it is snowing. Ask your friend how long ...
....

C I have been doing or I have done? (1–2)

Complete the conversation. Write the verbs in the Present Perfect or Present Perfect Progressive.

Adrienne: What are you doing, Ken? (►) You've been........ (you/be) in here for hours. You're making a huge mess.
Ken: (1) .... (I/clean) out this closet most of the afternoon. There's a lot of old stuff in here. (2) .... (I/find) these—look.
Adrienne: (3) .... (you/sit) there staring at those old skates for the last five minutes. (4) .... (I/watch) you. (5) .... (you/be) daydreaming.
Ken: They're my hockey skates. (6) .... (I/have) them since I was about sixteen. (7) .... (they/be) in here for years.
Adrienne: Well, throw them away. And what about that tennis racquet? Is that yours?
Ken: No, it must be yours. (8) .... (I/never/have) a tennis racquet.

Will and be going to

1 Introduction

Deepha: *It's my birthday soon.* ***I'll be*** *twenty next Friday.*
Grace: *Oh, really?* ***Are*** *you* ***going to have*** *a party?*
Deepha: ***I'm going to have*** *dinner in a restaurant with a few friends.*
Grace: *That'**ll be** nice.*

WILL

Will has a neutral meaning. We use it to talk about facts in the future.

*I'**ll be** twenty next Friday.*
*The space shuttle **will come** down in the Pacific Ocean tomorrow morning.*

BE GOING TO

We use **be going to** for an intention, something we have already decided to do.

*We'**re going to have** dinner.*
*Larry **is going to sell** his car.*

Will does <u>not</u> express an intention.

*It's her birthday. She'**s going to have** dinner with her friends.* NOT ~~*She'll have dinner.*~~

But we often use **be going to** for an intention and **will** for the details and comments.

*We'**re** all **going to have** dinner. There'**ll be** about ten of us. ~ Oh, that'**ll be** nice.*

As well as **be going to**, we can use the Present Progressive (see page 14).

*We'**re going to drive**/We'**re driving** down to Florida. ~ That'**ll be** a long trip. ~ Yes, it'**ll take** two days. We'**ll arrive** on Sunday.*

2 Decisions and intentions

WILL

We use **will** for an instant decision or agreement to do something.

*There's a mail box over there. I'**ll mail** these letters.*
*You still haven't fixed the door, Frank. ~ OK, I'**ll do** it tomorrow.*

Frank is deciding now.

BE GOING TO

Be going to means that we have already decided.

*I'm going out. I'**m going to mail** these letters.*
*You still haven't fixed the door, Frank. ~ I know. I'**m going to do** it tomorrow.*

Frank has already decided.

3 Predictions

WILL

We can use **will** for a prediction about the future.

*I think the Alouettes **will win** the game.*
*One day people **will travel** to Mars.*

BE GOING TO

We use **be going to** for a prediction when we see from the present situation what is going to happen in the future.

*There isn't a cloud in the sky. It'**s going to be** a lovely day.*
*This bag isn't very strong. It'**s going to break**.*

It is often possible to use either form in a prediction. For example, we can also say *I think the Alouettes **are going to win** the game.* Usually **be going to** is a little more informal and conversational than **will**.

Practice

A Will and be going to (1–2)

Complete the conversations. Write *will* or *be going to* with the verbs.

▶ Mila: Do you have a ticket for the play?
Jake: Yes, I'm going to see .... (see) it on Thursday.

▶ Rena: The alarm's going off. It's making an awful noise.
Yuki: OK, I'll turn .... (turn) it off.

1 Abbas: Did you buy this book?
Matthew: No, Emma did. She .... (read) it on vacation.

2 Ling: Would you like tea or coffee?
Jessie: Oh, I .... (have) coffee, please.

3 Nathan: I'm going to miss a good show on TV because I'll be out tonight.
Joe: I .... (record) it for you, if you like.

4 Lynda: I'm just going out to get a paper.
Betty: What newspaper .... (you/buy)?

B Will and be going to (1–3)

What would you say? Use *will* or *be going to*.

▶ You want to express your intention to look around the museum.
Your friend: Do you have any plans for this afternoon?
You: Yes, I'm going to look around the museum. ....

1 You hate dogs. Dogs always attack you if they get the chance.
Your friend: That dog doesn't look very friendly.
You: It's coming towards us. ....

2 You predict the landing of aliens on the earth in the next ten years.
Your friend: All this talk about aliens is complete nonsense, isn't it?
You: Is it? I think ....

3 You know that your friend's sister has decided to get married.
Your friend: Have you heard about my sister?
You: Well, I heard that ....

4 You suddenly decide you want to invite Jasmine out for dinner.
Your friend: Did you know that Jasmine will be in town next weekend?
You: No, I didn't. ....

C Will and be going to (1–3)

Complete the news report about the town of Vanderhoof.
Use *will* or *be going to*. Sometimes either is possible.

We have learned this week that the local council has plans for Westside Park in Vanderhoof. The council (▶) is going to sell .... (sell) the land to a builder, McDonald and Son. The plans are all set. "(1) .... (we/build) fifty houses," said Mr. McDonald. "In two years' time everything (2) .... (be) finished. I'm sure people (3) .... (like) the houses. Most of them (4) .... (be) for young families. And we intend to take care of the environment. (5) .... (we/not/cut) down all the trees, only a few of them." But people living near the park are angry. "This is a terrible idea. We're all against it," said Vena Patel. "(6) .... (we/have) a protest march on Saturday. I expect that everyone in Vanderhoof (7) .... (be) there. We've reached our decision. (8) .... (we/stop) this plan."

Present tenses for the future

1 Present Progressive for plans

Lazlo: ***Are** you **doing** anything this evening?*
Pavel: *Yes, **I'm going** to a hockey game.*
*The Leafs **are playing** the Senators.*
I bought my ticket yesterday.

We use the Present Progressive for what someone has arranged to do in the future.
Here Pavel plans to go to the game. (He has bought a ticket.)
Here are some more examples.

***I'm meeting** Marc at six o'clock.* — *David **is coming** to our place later on.*
***We're having** a party tomorrow.* — *Monique **is going** to Edmonton next week.*

We also use the Present Progressive to talk about things happening now.
Present: *We**'re having** a party **right now**.*
Future: *We**'re having** a party **tomorrow**.*
Here the phrase of time shows whether we mean the present or the future. But sometimes there is no phrase of time, as when Pavel says, "The Leafs are playing the Senators." Here it is clear from Lazlo's question that the conversation is about a future event.

The Present Progressive for the future and **be going to** have similar meanings.
*We**'re having** a party next week.* (We have made plans.)
*We**'re going to have** a party next week.* (We intend/We have decided to have one.)
Often we can use either form.
***I'm meeting/I'm going to meet** Marc at six o'clock.*

2 Simple Present for a timetable

Igor: *What time **does** your **train** leave tomorrow?*
Lynn: *Seven twenty-three in the morning.*
*It **gets** into Montreal at eleven twenty-three.*

We can use the Simple Present for the future when we are talking about a timetable, usually a public one such as a train timetable.
*The train **leaves** at seven twenty-three tomorrow morning.*
*The game **starts** at seven.*
*Next Friday **is** the thirteenth.*
*I've got the tour details here. We **spend** three days in Rome.*
Compare the Simple Present for repeated actions (see page 2).
*The train **leaves** at seven twenty-three **every morning**.*

3 Be to and be about to

We use **be to** for a future event that is officially arranged.
It is often used in news reports.
*The prime minister **is to visit** Iqaluit in November.*
*The Pan Am Games **are to take place** in Toronto next year.*
We could also use the Present Progressive here.
*The prime minister **is visiting** Iqaluit in November.*

We use **be about to** for the very near future.
*The plane is at the end of the runway. It **is about to take** off.*
*Do you want to say goodbye to our visitors? They**'re about to leave**.*

Practice

A Present Progressive (1)

Read the conversation and decide if the verb refers to the present or the future.

Diego: (▶) What <u>are</u> you <u>reading</u>, Carmella?
Carmella: Oh, it's a guidebook to Brazil. (1) I<u>'m going</u> there next month. (2) My sister and I <u>are taking</u> a vacation there. (3) I<u>'m</u> really <u>looking</u> forward to it. (4) We<u>'re spending</u> three weeks in Rio. (5) So I<u>'m finding</u> out about all the things we can do there.

▶ present .... 3 ....
1 .... 4 ....
2 .... 5 ....

B Present Progressive for plans (1)

For each situation, write a sentence with the Present Progressive. Use the verbs in parentheses.

▶ Scott and Sean have accepted an invitation to Su Lin's party next week. (go)
They're going to Su Lin's party next week. ....
1 Laura has agreed to be in the office on Saturday. (work)
....
2 Isabel has just bought a plane ticket to Cairo dated May 15. (fly)
....
3 Mitch has scheduled a meeting with his boss at four o'clock this afternoon. (see)
....
4 Roger and Sven have booked a tennis court for tomorrow afternoon. (play)
....

C Present tenses for the future (1–2)

Write the verbs in the Present Progressive or the Simple Present.

Raina: (▶) Are you doing .... (you/do) anything tonight?
James: Yes, (1) .... (I/go) to the airport to meet my friend Antonio. (2) .... (he/stay) here for the weekend, remember? His plane (3) .... (get) in at eight-fifteen.
Raina: Oh, of course. I'd forgotten about that.
James: Maybe we'll see you later. What (4) .... (you/do) tonight?
Raina: Oh, (5) .... (I/go) to the movies with Jen and Kaya and a couple of other people. The movie (6) .... (finish) pretty early, so (7) .... (we/go) to a pizza place afterwards.

D Be to and be about to (3)

Complete these sentences from the news. Some are spoken by the news anchor in the studio and some by reporters on the spot. Use *be to* or *be about to* with the verbs in parentheses.

▶ The new museum is to open .... (open) in the fall.
▶ The prime minister is at the microphone now. He is about to start .... (start) speaking.
1 The lead runner is almost there now. She .... (win) the race.
2 Taxes .... (go) up next April.
3 The US president .... (visit) Ottawa in the new year.
4 The riot isn't over yet, but the police are here. They .... (move) in.
5 The talks on world trade .... (take) place later this year.

Will be doing

1 Introduction

Shanti: *Would you like to come to our party tomorrow, Han?*

Han: *Thanks for the invitation, but I'm very busy at my job.* ***I'll be working*** *all day tomorrow.*

Shanti: *You* ***won't be working*** *on Saturday night, of course. Come on, Han, take a break.* *We'**ll be starting*** *at about ten o'clock.*

We can use **will be** + an **-ing** form (the Future Progressive) to talk about future actions. There are two different uses.

2 Will be doing for continuous actions

We use the Future Progressive for an action over a period of time.
It means that at some time in the future we will be in the middle of an action.

*Han can't go to the party. He***'ll be working** *all day tomorrow.*
I'll be out at three o'clock. ***I'll be playing*** *golf.*
When the men leave the building, the police **will be waiting** *for them.*
What **will** *we* **be doing** *in ten years' time, I wonder?*

Compare the Past Progressive, Present Progressive, and Future Progressive.

Past: *This time* ***last week*** *we* ***were sitting*** *on the beach.*
Present: ***Right now*** *we****'re sitting*** *on the beach.*
Future: *This time* ***next week*** *we****'ll be sitting*** *on the beach.*

Compare **will do** and **will be doing** in these sentences.

The band **will play** *when the prime minister enters.*
(The prime minister will enter and then the band will play.)
The band **will be playing** *when the prime minister enters.*
(The band will start playing before the prime minister enters.)

3 Will be doing for single actions

We also use **will be** + an **-ing** form for an action which will happen in the course of events because it is part of a plan or part of a schedule of future events.

The party **will be starting** *at ten o'clock.* (part of the evening's events)
The ship **will be sailing** *soon.* (part of our trip)

More than one form is often possible. **Will** and the Present Progressive (page 14) often have a very similar meaning.

The visitors ***will be arriving/will arrive/are arriving*** *later.*

We often use the Future Progressive for something that will happen as part of a routine.

I'll stop by and see you tomorrow afternoon. ***I'll be passing*** *your house. It's on my way home from work.*
Erin and Jack **will be cleaning** *the house tomorrow. They always do it on Sunday.*

We can also use **will be** + an **-ing** form to ask about someone's plans.

Will *you* ***be going*** *anywhere near a pharmacy this morning? ~ Yes, why? ~ Could you get me some aspirin, please? ~ Yes, of course.*
How long ***will*** *you* ***be using*** *this computer? ~ You can have it in a minute.*

Practice

A Will be doing (2)

Complete the conversation. Write a pronoun and the Future Progressive form of the verb.

Josh: I'm going to go into business when I finish university. Five years from now (▶) I'll be running............... (I/run) a big company. I expect (1) .... (I/earn) lots of money.

Christy: I don't know what (2) .... (I/do). What about you, Natasha? What (3) .... (you/do), do you think?

Natasha: I'm too lazy to do any work. I plan to marry someone very rich. (4) .... (I/host) dinner parties all the time. We'll have a cook (5) .... (who/do) all the work, of course. And you'll both get invitations.

Christy: You're joking, aren't you, Natasha? I think (6) .... (you/play) in an orchestra. That's what you really want to do, isn't it?

B Will be doing (3)

Write the answers. People are saying what they will be doing as part of their routine.

▶ Marc: When are you going to the club? (Jacob goes to the club every Friday.)
Jacob: I'll be going there next Friday...

1 Bella: Are you likely to see Janette in the near future? (Bella sees Janette every day.)
Bella: .... tomorrow.

2 Marie: Are you going to Nova Scotia again soon? (Henri goes to Nova Scotia every summer.)
Henri: ....

3 Jessica: When are you going to play badminton again? (Mathieu plays badminton every weekend.)
Mathieu: ....

4 Jason: When are you next having lunch in the cafeteria? (Alvaro has lunch in the cafeteria every day.)
Alvaro: ....

C Will be doing (3)

You want to ask a friend to do something for you or to let you do something. Find out if it is convenient for your friend. Use the verbs in parentheses.

▶ You want to borrow your friend's magazine tonight. (read)
Will you be reading your magazine tonight?......................................

1 You want your friend to take your library book back today. (go to)
....

2 You want your friend to send your best wishes to Alyssa soon. (write to)
....

3 You want to use your friend's calculator this afternoon. (use)
....

4 You want your friend to give a photo to Daniel tomorrow. (see)
....

5 You want your friend to give you a ride to the concert. (drive)
....

6 You want your friend to give a message to her sister soon. (call)
....

Short forms (**it's, don't**)

1 The use of short forms

A short form like **it's** or **don't** stands for the full form **it is** or **do not.** We leave out one or more letters and we write an apostrophe (') instead. We use short forms in conversational English and in informal writing such as a letter to a friend. Short forms are sometimes called "contracted forms."

We cannot use a short form when the word is stressed, in a short answer for example.
Have you looked in this drawer? ~ Yes, I ***have.*** NOT ~~*Yes, I've.*~~
But we can use **n't** in a short answer: *No, I* ***haven't.***

2 The most common short forms

Some verbs can have short forms when they come after **I**, **you**, etc.

VERB	SHORT FORMS
am	I'm
are	you're, we're, they're
is/has	he's, she's, it's
have	I've, you've, we've, they've
had/would	I'd, you'd, he'd, she'd, it'd, we'd, they'd
will	I'll, you'll, he'll, she'll, it'll, we'll, they'll
shall	I'll, we'll

A short form can also come after a noun.
Mabel's *lost her bank card.* (Mabel **has** ...) *The* ***card'll*** *be in here.* (The card **will** ...)

There are also some short forms with question words and with **here**, **there**, or **that.**

who's, what's, where's, when's, how's, who'd, who'll, what'll
here's, there's, that's, there'll, that'll, there'd, that'd

There is a negative short form **n't** which can come after some verbs.

aren't, isn't, wasn't, weren't, haven't, hasn't, hadn't, don't /dəʊnt/, doesn't, didn't, won't (= will not), shan't (= shall not), can't /kɑːnt/, couldn't, shouldn't, wouldn't

Sometimes we can shorten either **not** or the verb.
It is not *funny.* → ***It isn't*** *funny. or* ***It's not*** *funny.*
You will not *believe it.* → ***You won't*** *believe it.* OR ***You'll not*** *believe it.*
But we cannot use **n't** after **I**.
I am not *sure.* → ***I'm not*** *sure.* NOT ~~*I amn't sure.*~~

3 's and 'd

's can be **is** or **has,** and **'d** can be **had** or **would.**
She's short, and she's got fair hair. (She **is** short ... she **has** got ...)
If I'd known, I'd have told you. (If I **had** known, I **would** have ...)

Practice

A Short forms (2)

Write the sentences in a more informal style, with short forms.

In a business email	In an email to a friend
▶ You are absolutely right.	You're absolutely right.
1 It is a difficult problem.	....
2 I have seen the results.	....
3 I do not have any information.	....
4 We have not reached a decision.	....
5 I am very excited about it.	....
6 You do not need to decide now.	....
7 It is not yet certain.	....
8 We will be happy to see you.	....
9 Do not worry.	....
10 I would like to buy a new computer.	....
11 We are willing to help.	....
12 We will not know the result for some time.	....

B Short forms (2)

Complete the dialogues. Write the short form of these phrases:
do not, he is, ~~I am~~, is not, it is, what is, where is

▶

1

2

3

▶ How are you? ~ I'm........... fine, thanks.
1 .... your luggage? ~ .... in Los Angeles.
2 Do you like this shirt? ~ No, I .... It .... my style.
3 .... that smell? ~ My husband. .... doing a science experiment.

C 's and 'd (3)

Write the full forms. Use *is*, *has*, *had*, or *would*.

▶ What's your name?	What is your name?
1 I'd like a coffee, please.	....
2 There's been an accident.	....
3 That's correct.	....
4 I'd seen the movie before.	....
5 Who's got the key?	....
6 We'd have stopped if we'd seen you.	....

Wh- questions

1 Introduction

Reporter Helena Papadopoulos is interviewing some guerrilla fighters.

Helena:	Guerrillas:
***Why** are you fighting?*	*For our freedom.*
***What** can you do for the people?*	*We can help them.*
***When** will the war be over?*	*Very soon.*

A **wh**- question begins with a question word. Question words are **who, what, which, whose, where, when, why**, and **how**. We use a **wh**- question to ask for information.

2 Form

Most **wh**- questions begin with a question word + an auxiliary verb + the subject. An auxiliary verb is a form of **be** or **have** or a modal verb, e.g. **can**.

QUESTION WORD	AUXILIARY	SUBJECT	VERB
What	**is**	**Helena**	doing?
Where	**have**	**you**	travelled?
When	**can**	**we**	travel safely?

The main verb **be** also comes before the subject in questions.

*Where **is** Helena?* *How **are** you?* *What **was** that noise?*

If there is more than one auxiliary verb, only the first one comes before the subject.

*The guerrillas **have been** hiding.* → *Where **have** the guerrillas been hiding?*

*I **should have** said something.* → *What **should** I have said?*

In the Simple Present and Simple Past we use a form of **do**.

QUESTION WORD	AUXILIARY	SUBJECT	VERB
Where	**do**	**people**	meet?
How	**does**	**the radio**	work?
What	**did**	**the guerrillas**	say?

An ordinary verb such as **meet, work**, or **say** cannot come before the subject.

NOT ~~*Where meet people?*~~ and NOT ~~*How works the radio?*~~

The verb after the subject does not end in **-s** or **-ed**.

NOT ~~*How does the radio works?*~~ and NOT ~~*What did the guerrillas said?*~~

3 Question phrases

Look at these question phrases with **what** and **how**.

***What time** is your friend arriving? ~ Eight-thirty.* ***What colour** is your toothbrush? ~ Yellow.*

***What kind of/What sort of** club is it? ~ A dance club.* ***How old** is your sister? ~ She's twenty.*

***How often** do you go out? ~ About once a week, usually.* ***How far** is the beach? ~ Only a five-minute walk.*

***How long** will the meeting last? ~ An hour or so, I believe.* ***How many** televisions do you have? ~ Three.*

***How much** money did you spend? ~ About a hundred dollars.*

Practice

A Wh- questions (1–2)

What would you say in these situations?

► You are talking to a man at a party. Ask him where he works.
Where do you work?

1 You want to know what the date is today. Ask your friend.
....

2 You've forgotten what time your class ends. Ask your friend.
....

3 Your friend is having a party. You'd like to know who he has invited. Ask him.
....

4 Your favourite band is going to play a concert. Ask how you can get tickets.
....

5 You are downtown with a friend, and you are wondering where the two of you are going to have lunch. What do you ask?
....

B Question words and phrases (1–3)

Game-show champion Philippe LaFleur is answering questions. Write these words and phrases: ***how far*, *how long*, *how often*, *how many*, *what*, ~~*what colour*~~, *what kind*, *when*, *where*, *who***

	Game-show host:		**Claude:**
►	*What colour*	is the Greek flag?	Blue and white.
1	....	is Melbourne?	It's in Australia.
2	....	centimetres are there in a kilometre?	A hundred thousand.
3	....	did the Second World War end?	In 1945.
4	....	did Romeo love?	Juliet.
5	....	is Sirius?	It's a star.
6	....	is it from Vancouver to Calgary?	About 1000 kilometres.
7	....	are the Winter Olympics held?	Every four years.
8	....	of food is cheddar?	It's cheese.
9	....	is a hockey game?	Sixty minutes.

C Wh- questions (1–3)

Javier is interviewing a guest on his talk show. It's the actress Ruby Patel, who is on the soap opera *Love in the Arctic*. Write Javier's questions.

► Javier: *How often do you tape Love in the Arctic?*
Ruby: Oh, we tape it every day. It's a full-time job, you know.

1 Javier: And .... it?
Ruby: In Toronto, at the Can-TV studio.

2 Javier: ....
Ruby: How many? Well, let me see, I think we've done a thousand episodes.

3 Javier: ....
Ruby: I'm not going to tell you. How much money I earn is my business.

4 Javier: OK, I'm sorry. ....
Ruby: Oh, a long time ago. I started acting when I was twelve.

5 Javier: ....
Ruby: My plans for the future? I just want to go on with *Love in the Arctic*.

Prepositions in wh- questions

1 Introduction

Gerry and Angel each ask Claudette a question. In each question, the word **what** is the object of a preposition (**for**, **about**).

__What__ are you looking __for__?
(You are looking **for something**.)
__What__ are you worrying __about__?
(You are worrying **about something**.)

The preposition normally comes in the same place as in a statement: **looking for, worrying about.**

NOT ~~*For what are you looking?*~~
NOT ~~*About what are you worrying?*~~

But in more formal English, the preposition can come before the question word.

__In which__ warehouse were the goods stored?
OR *__Which__ warehouse were the goods stored __in__?*

In formal English we use a preposition + whom (not ***who***).

__From whom__ did you obtain the information?
OR *__Whom__ did you obtain the information __from__?*

However, you will not commonly hear *whom* used in spoken English.

Here are some more examples of prepositions in **wh-** questions.

__Whom__ are we waiting __for__? ~ Sandy.
__What's__ Nick laughing __at__? ~ Oh, one of Patrick's jokes.
__Where__ are you __from__?/__Where__ do you come __from__? ~ Fredericton.
__What kind of__ vacation are you interested __in__? ~ An all-inclusive trip.
__Whom__ did you go out __with__ last night? ~ Just a friend.

2 What ... for and what ... like

We can use a question with **what ... for** to ask about purpose.

__What__ did you buy this computer magazine __for__? ~ To read about business software.
__What__ are these bricks __for__? ~ We're going to build a wall.
__What__ are they digging the road up __for__? ~ They're repairing a gas pipe.

What ... for means the same as **why**.

__Why__ are they digging up the road? ~ They're repairing a gas pipe.

We can use **what ... like** to ask if something is good or bad, interesting or boring, etc.

__What__ was the party __like__? ~ Oh, we had a great time.
__What__'s the place where you live __like__? ~ It's pretty quiet.

Note also **look like.**

__What__ does your friend __look like__? ~ She's very tall and blond.

But we use **how** to ask about someone's well-being.

__How__ are you? ~ I'm OK, thanks. And you?
__How__ are you doing at your new job? ~ I'm really enjoying it.

Compare these two questions.

__How__'s Pinder? ~ Oh, she's fine, thanks. (She is happy/in good health.)
__What__'s Pinder __like__? ~ She's very nice. (She is a nice person.)

Practice

A Prepositions in wh- questions (1)

Ask these people questions with *what*.
Use these verbs and prepositions: *look at*, *~~look for~~*, *point at*, *talk about*, *wait for*

▶ What are you looking for?
1 ....
2 ....
3 ....
4 ....

B Prepositions in wh- questions (1)

Write the question. Use *what* and put the preposition in parentheses at the end.

▶ Jasmine: Aaron is smiling. He's pleased. (about)
Vytas: Yes, he is. What is he pleased about?
▶ Jay: I'm busy today. I'm getting ready. (for)
Travis: What are you getting ready for?
1 Jessica: I've done something awful. I'm ashamed. (of)
Brett: ....
2 Virginia: Haven't you heard of Rita MacNeil? She's famous. (for)
Karen: No, I haven't. ....
3 Sian: Marc is annoyed. He's going to complain. (about)
Jesse: ....
4 Phoebe: Greta's in a hurry. She's going to be late. (for)
Jeff: ....
5 Olivia: I don't feel very relaxed. I feel nervous. (about)
Rudy: ....

C What ... for and what ... like (2)

Trevor has just come home from work. Complete the conversation. Write *for*, *how*, *like*, or *what*.

Riyaad: Hello, dear. (▶) ......How...... are you?
Emili: Hello. I'm all right, but I'm in a bit of a rush getting ready for the barbecue.
Riyaad: Um, I forgot to tell you that I invited two more people.
Emili: (1) .... are you telling me now (2) .... ? I've bought all the food. I just hope there's enough. Anyway, who are these people? (3) .... are they (4) .... ?
Riyaad: They're friends of James. They're very nice people. And after all, (5) .... are parties (6) .... ? To meet new people.
Emili: It isn't a party, it's a barbecue. (7) .... 's the weather going to be (8) .... ?
Riyaad: The forecast said it's going to be perfect. Warm and dry.
Emili: Good. And (9) .... was your day?
Riyaad: Oh, not too bad. Busy as usual.

Negative statements

1 Use

John Cabot

*John Cabot was a famous Italian explorer. Some people believe that he "discovered" Canada, but this **isn't** true. Cabot **was not** the first European to arrive in Canada—the Vikings had sailed here almost five centuries earlier, around the year 1000. Other Europeans may have arrived before then, but we **don't** know for sure. People are also unsure of where exactly Cabot landed. He probably landed in Newfoundland or Nova Scotia. Regardless of when or where he landed, Aboriginals had already lived here for thousands of years, long before any European explorers landed in this country. So, Cabot **didn't** discover Canada.*

We often use a negative statement to correct a mistaken idea, such as the idea that John Cabot discovered Canada.

2 Negative verb forms

	POSITIVE	NEGATIVE	
be:	*are dancing*	***are not** dancing*	OR ***aren't** dancing*
have:	***have** seen*	***have not** seen*	OR ***haven't** seen*
Modal verb:	***could** stay*	***could not** stay*	OR ***couldn't** stay*

In a negative statement **not** or **n't** comes after the auxiliary verb.
The auxiliary verb is a form of **be**, **have**, or a modal verb, e.g. **must**, **can**, **could**.

*The girls **are not** dancing. The phone **isn't** working properly.*
*I **haven't** seen the new Pixar movie. David **hasn't** been at school this week.*
*I **shouldn't** stay long. You **can't** turn right here.*
***I'm not** feeling very awake today.*

We write **n't** without a space between it and the verb that comes before it, e.g. **isn't**, **haven't**.

Not or **n't** also comes after the main verb **be**.

*The muffins **are not** ready yet. It **isn't** very warm in here.*

If there is more than one auxiliary verb, we put **not** or **n't** after the first one.

*This plate **hasn't** been washed. You **shouldn't** have bothered.*

In the Simple Present and Simple Past, we use a form of **do**.

	POSITIVE	NEGATIVE	
Simple Present:	*work*	***do not** work*	OR ***don't** work*
	looks	***does not** look*	OR ***doesn't** look*
Simple Past:	*enjoyed*	***did not** enjoy*	OR ***didn't** enjoy*

*I **don't** work on Saturdays.* NOT ~~*I work not on Saturdays.*~~
*This painting **doesn't** look very nice. I'm afraid we **didn't** enjoy the trip very much.*

The verb after **not** or **n't** does not end in **-s** or **-ed**.

NOT ~~*It doesn't looks very nice*~~ and NOT ~~*We didn't enjoyed the trip.*~~

3 No and not

We can use **no** before a noun or an adjective + noun. The verb is positive.

***No** music is allowed after eleven.* OR *Music is not allowed after eleven.*
*There are **no** new houses in the town.* OR *There aren't any new houses in the town.*

We do not use **no** with a verb.

NOT ~~*Music is no allowed*~~ and NOT ~~*The stores are no open.*~~

Practice

A Use (1)

Read the information about John Cabot in part 1.
Then choose a positive or a negative verb.

▶ Cabot ~~discovered~~/didn't discover Canada.
1 The first European to sail to Canada was/wasn't Cabot.
2 Europeans had/hadn't been to Canada before Cabot.
3 We know/don't know definitely who first sailed to Canada.
4 Cabot landed/didn't land in British Columbia.
5 People today are/aren't sure where he landed.
6 Aboriginals lived/didn't live here for a long time before Cabot arrived.

B Negative verb forms (1)

Complete the conversation, Write the negative forms of these words:
can*, *did*, *do*, *does*, *have*, *is*, *was*, *were

Faizal: Does anyone live in that house next door?
Eugenia: Yes, his name is Jake. He's kind of strange. He (▶) doesn't have a job, but he (1) .... be short of money because he just bought a new car.
Faizal: The house (2) .... look very well maintained.
Eugenia: The people who lived there before Jake (3) .... look after it very well. And they (4) .... very good at gardening. When Jake bought the house, it had been empty for a while. It (5) .... very expensive. But he (6) .... interested in doing anything to it, as you can see.
Faizal: Is he a friend?
Eugenia: No, we aren't really friends. I (7) .... know him very well. I say hello when I see him, that's all. I (8) .... seen him for a while, actually.

C Negative verb forms (2)

Marisol and Kara are good friends, but they are very different kinds of people.
Complete the sentences using a negative.

▶ Marisol gets upset, but Kara doesn't get upset.
1 Marisol gets headaches. Kara is lucky. She ....
2 Kara can relax. Marisol is different. She ....
3 Kara missed a lecture yesterday, but Marisol ....
4 Marisol is a nervous person, but Kara ....
5 Marisol loses things. Kara ....
6 Kara was a happy child. Marisol ....
7 Kara has decided on a career, but Marisol ....

D No and not (3)

Complete this paragraph from a travel article. Write *no* or *not*.

Metropolis is (▶) not an attractive town. There are (1) .... parks or gardens downtown. I saw (2) .... interesting buildings—only factories, offices, and apartment buildings. The hotels are (3) .... very good, and there are (4) .... fine-dining restaurants. (5) .... tourists visit Metropolis, and I certainly do (6) .... want to go there again.

Ability: **can, could, and be able to**

1 Can and **can't**

Matthew: *How many instruments **can** you play, Arvid?*
Arvid: *Three—the violin, the clarinet, and the piano.*
Matthew: *That's terrific. You don't have a piano here, though.*
Arvid: *No, but I **can** go to the music room in college and play the one in there.*
Matthew: *I'm not musical at all. I **can't** even sing.*

We use **can** to say that something is possible: that someone has an ability (*Arvid **can** play the piano*) or an opportunity (*He **can** go to the music room*). **Can** is usually pronounced /kən/ but sometimes we say /kæn/. The negative is **cannot** /ˈkænɒt/ or **can't** /kɑːnt/.

2 Can and **be able to**

In the present tense, **be able to** is a little more formal and less usual than **can**.

*Emma is good with computers. She **can** write/**is able to** write codes.*

But in some structures we always use **be able to**, not **can**.

To-infinitive:	*It's nice **to be able to go** to the opera.* (NOT ~~*to can go*~~)
After a modal verb:	*Josh **might be able to** help us.*
Present Perfect:	*It's been quiet today. **I've been able to** get some work done.*

For the future we use **can** or **will be able to** but NOT ~~*will can*~~.

*If we earn some money, we **can** go/**we'll be able to** go on vacation next summer.*
*I'm afraid I **can't** come/I **won't be able to** go to the party on Friday.*

But to suggest a possible future action, we normally use **can**.

*Let's have lunch together. We **can** go to that new restaurant.*

3 Could and **was/were able to**

For ability or opportunity in the past, we use **could** or **was/were able to**.

*Glenis **could** play (*OR *was able to** play) the piano when she was four.*
*In those days we had a car, so we **could** travel (*OR ***were able to** travel) very easily.*

To say that the ability or opportunity resulted in a particular action—something that really happened—we use **was/were able to** but not **could**.

*The plane **was able to** take off at eleven o'clock, after the fog had lifted.*
*Luckily, Mark **was able to** get (*OR *succeeded in getting) the work done in time.*
*The drivers **were able to** stop (*OR *managed to stop) before they crashed into each other.*

Compare these two sentences.

*The children **could** swim when they were very young.* (a past ability)	*The children **were able** to swim across the river.* (a past action)

In negative sentences and questions, we can use either form.

*It was snowing heavily, so the plane **couldn't/wasn't able** to take off.*
*The pool was closed, so they **couldn't/weren't able to** go swimming.*
***Could you/Were** you **able to** describe the man to the police?*

We normally use **could** (not **was/were able to**) with verbs of seeing etc., and with verbs of thinking.

*We **could see** the city in the distance.*
*As soon as Vina opened the door, she **could smell** gas.*
*I **couldn't understand** what was happening.*

Practice

A Can and can't (1)

Look at the pictures and say what they can or can't do. Use these words: *climb trees*, *juggle*, *lift the weights*, *play the violin*, ~~*walk on his hands*~~

▶ 

1 

2 

3 

4 

▶ He can walk on his hands.

1 ....

2 ....

3 ....

4 ....

B Can and be able to (2)

Luca is visiting Emmanuel, who hurt himself when he fell off a ladder. Complete the conversation using *can* or a form of *be able to*. Sometimes there is more than one possible answer.

Luca: Hello, Emmanuel. I'm sorry I haven't (▶) been able to come......... (come) and see you before. I've been really busy lately. How are you?

Emmanuel: I'm OK, thanks. (1) .... (I/walk) around now. The doctor says (2) .... (I/go) back to work soon. It'll be nice (3) .... (get) out again. I hate being stuck here like this. I haven't (4) .... (do) anything fun.

C Could and was/were able to (3)

▶ **Which is closer to the meaning of the sentence "Years ago I could run a marathon"?**

a) ☐ I ran a marathon at one particular time in the past.

b) ☑ I was once in good enough shape to run a very long way.

1 **Which of these sentences is correct?**

I was sick, so I couldn't go to the party.

I was sick, so I wasn't able to go to the party.

a) ☐ Only the first one. b) ☐ Only the second one. c) ☐ Both of them.

2 **Which is closer to the meaning of the sentence "Sarah was able to leave work early yesterday"?**

a) ☐ Sarah left work early yesterday.

b) ☐ Sarah had the opportunity to leave work early yesterday, but we don't know if she took it.

D Could and was/were able to (3)

Write *could* or *was/were able to*. Sometimes either is possible. Use a negative if necessary.

▶ Suddenly, all the lights went out. We couldn't............ see a thing.

1 The computer wasn't working, but luckily Anne-Marie .... fix it.

2 There was a big party last night. You .... hear the music a kilometre away.

3 I learned to read music as a child. I .... read it when I was five.

4 People heard warnings about the flood, and they .... move out in time.

5 The train was full. I .... find a seat anywhere.

Possibility and certainty: **may, might, could, must, etc.**

1 May, might, and could

Evan: *Whose purse is that?*
Janna: *I don't know. It **may** belong to Maria's friend.*
Craig: *It **might** be a bomb. It **could** explode at any moment.*

We use **may** or **might** to say that something is possible or that it is quite likely. We can use them for the present or the future.

*It **may/might** be a bomb.* (= Perhaps it is a bomb.)
*I **may/might** go to the bar tomorrow.* (= Perhaps I will go to the bar.)

We can use **could** to say that something is possible.

*The story **could** be true, I suppose.* (= Possibly it is true.)
*You **could** win a million dollars!* (= Possibly you will win a million dollars.)

Sometimes **could** means only a small possibility. It is possible (but not likely) that you will win a million dollars.

In some situations we can use **may**, **might**, or **could**.

*It **may/might/could** snow later.*

After **may**, **might**, or **could** we can use a progressive form (**be** + an **-ing** form).

*That man **may/might be watching** us.* (= Perhaps he is watching us.)
*Sharida **may/might be working** late tonight.* (= Perhaps she will be working late.)
*I'm not sure where Tang is. He **could be playing** squash.* (= Possibly he is playing squash.)

2 May, might, and could in the negative

The negative forms are **may not**, **might not**, and **could not/couldn't**.

MAY NOT AND MIGHT NOT	COULDN'T
Something negative is possible. *Vance **may not** get the job.* *Jin **might not** be home.* *I **might not** finish the marathon tomorrow.* (It is possible that I will not finish it.)	Something is impossible. *Lori is afraid of heights. She **couldn't** climb onto the roof.* *I'm completely out of shape. I **couldn't** run a marathon.* (It is impossible for me to run it.)

3 Must and can't

MUST	CAN'T
We use **must** when we realize that something is definitely true. *She isn't answering the phone. She **must** be out.* *I had my keys a minute ago. They **must** be here somewhere.* *Andrew isn't here. He **must** be working in the library.*	We use **can't** when we realize that something is impossible. *We haven't walked far. You **can't** be tired yet.* *Sleeping on that old mattress **can't** be comfortable.* *Jack **can't** be on vacation. I saw him here this morning.*

Practice

A Might be and might be doing (1)

Bob and Pat are at college. They're looking for their friend Heidi. Complete the conversation. Use *may* or *might* and the verb in parentheses. Sometimes you need to use the progressive form.

Bob: I can't find Heidi. Have you seen her?
Pat: (▶) She might be (she / be) in the music room. (▶) She may be practising (she/practise).
Bob: No, she isn't there. I thought (1) .... (she/be) with you.
Pat: It's a nice day. (2) .... (she/be) on the lawn.
(3) .... (she/sit) out there reading the paper. Or
(4) .... (she/have) a coffee.
(5) .... (you/find) her in the canteen.
Bob: No, I've looked there.
Pat: Well, here comes Jessica. (6) .... (she/know).

B May and might (1–2)

Add a sentence with *may* or *might* (both are correct).

▶ I'm not sure if it's going to rain. It might rain.
▶ I don't know if we'll see an elephant. We may see one.
1 I can't say whether Dave will win. ....
2 I haven't decided if I'm taking a vacation. ....
3 I don't know if we'll get an invitation. ....
4 I have no idea whether Chantal will be late. ....
5 I'm not sure if my friends are visiting me. ....

C Might not and could not (2)

Write *might not* or *could not/couldn't*.

▶ I've got one or two things to do, so I might not have time to come out tonight.
▶ David could not work as a taxi driver. He can't drive.
1 We're going to need lots of glasses. We .... have enough, you know.
2 Lars .... be in the office tomorrow. He thinks he's getting a cold.
3 We .... possibly get a dog, living in a small apartment like this.
4 How can you work with all this noise? I .... work in these conditions.
5 Don't come tomorrow because I .... be in. I'm not sure what I'm doing.

D Must, can't, and might (1, 3)

A reporter is interviewing Ms. Rizan for the evening news.
Complete the conversation. Write *must*, *can't*, or *might*.

Ms. Rizan: My name's Jen Rizan, and I'm going to go skydiving.
Reporter: Ms. Rizan, you're seventy-three, and you're going to jump out of an airplane. You (▶) must be crazy. You (1) .... be serious.
Ms. Rizan: It really (2) .... be wonderful to look down from the sky. I've always wanted to try it.
Reporter: But anything could happen. You (3) .... be injured or even killed. I wouldn't take the risk.
Ms. Rizan: Well, young man, your life (4) .... be much fun if you never take risks. You ought to try it. You never know—you (5) .... enjoy it.
Reporter: Enjoy it? You (6) .... be joking!

Should, ought to, had better, and be supposed to

1 Introduction

2 Should and ought to

We use **should** and **ought to** to say what is the best thing or the right thing to do. There is no difference in meaning, although **should** is much more common.

You're not feeling well. Perhaps you ***should*** *see a doctor.*
Your uncle was very nice to me. I ***ought to*** *write him a thank-you letter.*
People ***shouldn't*** *break their promises.*

We can also use **should** and **ought to** in questions to ask for advice.

Where do you think I ***should*** *put this picture?*
It's a difficult problem. How do you think we ***ought to*** *deal with it?*

After **should** or **ought to** we can use a progressive form (**be** + an **-ing** form).

It's six-thirty already. I ***should be making*** *dinner.*
Why are you sitting here doing nothing? You ***ought to be working****.*

3 Had better

We use **had better** to say what is the best thing to do in a situation.

It's cold. The children ***had better*** *wear their coats.*
*The neighbours are complaining. We****'d better*** *turn the music down.*
My wife is waiting for me. ***I'd better not*** *be late.*

We could also use **should** or **ought to** in these examples, although **had better** is stronger. The speaker sees the action as necessary and expects that it will happen.

4 Be supposed to

We use **be supposed to** when we are talking about the normal or correct way of doing things.

The guests ***are supposed to*** *buy flowers for the hostess.*
Look at these cars. This area ***is supposed to*** *be kept free of traffic.*
*The bus driver needs to concentrate. You****'re not supposed to*** *talk to him.*
How ***am*** *I* ***supposed to*** *cook this? ~ It tells you on the box.*

We can use **was/were supposed to** for the past.

It's eleven o'clock. You ***were supposed to*** *be here at ten-thirty, you know.*

Practice

A Should and ought to (2)

Write *should*, *shouldn't*, *ought*, or *ought not*. (Look for the word *to*.)

Marvin: I can't go out tonight, Paul. I (▶) ought .... to do some more work. I'm behind with everything. I've got so much to do.

Paul: You (1) .... worry so much, Marvin. Don't panic. You (2) .... to relax sometimes. You (3) .... take a break.

Marvin: I know I (4) .... panic, but I do. I can't help it.

Paul: Anyway, you're doing OK, aren't you? Your marks have been good. You (5) .... be happy. You (6) .... to invent problems for yourself.

B Had better (3)

What would you say in these situations? Add a sentence with *'d better* (*not*) and the words in parentheses.

▶ Marta doesn't feel well. She has a headache. What might you say to her? (a pain reliever)
You'd better take a pain reliever. ....

1 You and Jean are meeting Clara. You've both arrived, but she isn't there yet. She is usually late. (wait) ....

2 Yvonne is leaving her bike outside the recreation centre. You know it won't be safe if she leaves it unlocked. (lock) ....

3 Some friends are going to visit you today. Your room is in a mess. What do you think? (clean) ....

4 Todd is giving you a lift in his old sports car. There's a speed limit, and there's a police car behind you. (too fast) ....

5 There's an exam tomorrow. Neither you nor Monica have prepared for it. (some studying) ....

C Be supposed to (4)

Add a sentence using *be* (*not*) *supposed to* and these words:
~~leave it outside~~*, *report to the police*, *stand in a lineup*, *take two before meals*, *watch it

▶ You shouldn't bring your bike in here. You're supposed to leave it outside. ....

1 I've got some pills. ....

2 Foreign visitors can't travel freely here. ....

3 Be careful waiting for a bus in Canada. ....

4 This movie isn't for anyone under 18. ....

D Should, ought to, had better, and be supposed to (1–4)

Complete the conversation. Use *should*, *ought to*, *had better*, or *be supposed to* and the verbs in parentheses. Usually there is more than one correct answer.

Janis: What time (▶) are we supposed to be .... (we/be) at the morning meeting?

Courtland: The invitation says ten o'clock.

Janis: Well, it's ten now. (1) .... (we/hurry). (2) .... (we/not/be) late.

Courtland: Oh, it won't matter if we're a bit late.

Janis: I think it would be rude, wouldn't it? I don't think people (3) .... (arrive) late when they've been invited to something.

Courtland: You worry too much. (4) .... (you/not/take) everything so seriously, Janis. It's a casual meeting, not a job interview. (5) .... (we/not/get) there exactly on time.

Asking people to do things

1 Polite requests

We can use **can** or **could** in a request, when we ask someone to do something.

__Can__ you keep me informed? ~ Yes, of course.

__Could__ you lend me ten dollars until tomorrow? ~ Sorry, I don't have ten dollars.

I wonder if you __could__ explain something to me. ~ I'll try.

Could is often more polite than **can.**

In a request we can also use **Do you mind ...?** or **Would you mind...?** with an **-ing** form.

__Do you mind waiting__ a moment? ~ No, I can wait.

__Would you mind sitting__ in the back? ~ No, not at all.

We can also use **Would you like to ...?**

__Would you like to__ set the table for me? ~ Yes, of course.

We do not use **Do you like ...?** for a request. NOT ~~*Do you like to set the table for me?*~~

It is always worth taking the trouble to use one of these request forms in English. We do not normally say ~~*Set the table for me.*~~ This can sound very abrupt and impolite without a phrase like **Could you ...?**

2 The imperative

We can sometimes use the imperative form to tell someone what to do.

__Bring__ another chair. *__Hurry__ up or we'll be late.*

We form the negative with **don't.**

__Don't be__ silly. *__Don't make__ so much noise.*

We can use an imperative when we are with friends in an informal situation. But we do not use it to tell a stranger what to do in a more formal situation.

Excuse me. __Could you__ tell me how to get to Robson Street, please?

__Would you mind__ sending me a copy of your catalogue?

NOT ~~*Send me a copy of your catalogue.*~~

Even people in authority often avoid using the imperative to give orders. Instead they can use **I want/I'd like you to ...**, **You must ...**, or a polite request form.

Manager: *__I want you__ all to be at the meeting.*

Police officer: *__You must__ wait until you see the green light.*

Doctor: *__Could you__ lie down on the examination table, please?*

But we use an imperative in instructions and directions, in offers and invitations, and to express good wishes.

__Turn__ right at the intersection. *__Have__ a doughnut.*

__Enjoy__ your vacation.

3 Asking for things

We use **Can I/we have...?** and **Could I/we have ...?** when we ask someone to give us something.

__Can we have__ our room key, please? *__Could I have__ a receipt, please?*

We can also say *Could you give me a receipt, please?* but we do not use the imperative.

When we ask for something in a store or a restaurant, we can simply name what we want, but we must say **please.**

A whole-grain loaf, __please__. *Two coffees, __please__.*

We can also use **I'd like ...** or **I'll have ...**

__I'd like__ a chicken sandwich, please. *__I'll have__ a coffee.*

Practice

A Asking people to do things (1–3)

Complete these sentences and write them in: *Can I ... a fork, please? Could ... have a towel, ...? ~~Could you ... the ... for me?~~ Would you ... answering the phone?*

▶ 

1 

2 

3 

▶ Could you open the door for me?

1 ....

2 ....

3 ....

B Asking people to do things (1–3)

Mr. Noorani is the boss at Zedco. He tells everyone what to do. Complete his sentences.
Use these words: ***can, could, have, like, ~~mind~~, must, want, wonder, would***

▶ Would you mind .... making some coffee, Alain?
1 You .... inform me of any developments.
2 Could I .... the latest sales figures, please?
3 Would you .... to schedule a meeting some time next week, Fiona?
4 I .... everyone to read the report.
5 .... I see the file, please, Joel?
6 .... you mind putting this in writing?
7 I .... if you could translate this letter, Linda.
8 .... you meet our customer at the airport?

C Asking people to do things (1–3)

Read about each situation and then make a request. Use the word in parentheses.

▶ It is cold in the restaurant. Ask the waiter to close the window. (could)
Could you close the window, please?

1 You are buying a coat. Ask the sales clerk for a receipt. (can)
....

2 You want to know the time. Ask someone on the sidewalk. (could)
Excuse me. ....

3 You need someone to help you. Ask a friend. (can)
....

4 You have bought some groceries, but you don't have a bag. Ask the cashier for one. (could)
....

5 You are carrying a tray. Ask someone to clear a space on the table. (mind)
....

6 You are on the phone. You want to speak to the manager. (could)
....

Active and passive (1)

1 What is the sentence about?

Compare these two entries in an encyclopedia.

> **Alexander Graham Bell**
> A British inventor who went to live in Canada and then the US. Bell invented the telephone.

> **Telephone**
> An apparatus with which people can talk to each other over long distances. The telephone was invented by Alexander Graham Bell.

Look at these two sentences.

ACTIVE	PASSIVE
Bell *invented the telephone.*	***The telephone*** *was invented by Bell.*

The two sentences have the same meaning, but they are about different things. One sentence is about Bell, and the other is about the telephone. Each sentence begins with the subject. The subject is the starting-point of the sentence, the thing we are talking about. The new information about the subject comes at the end of the sentence.

We say *Bell invented the telephone* because we are talking about **Bell**, and the new information is that he invented **the telephone**.

When the subject is the person or thing doing the action (the agent), then we use an active verb.

ACTIVE

Bell *invented the telephone.*
(*Bell* = Subject and agent)

The subject (**Bell**) is the agent.

We say *The telephone was invented by Bell* because we are talking about **the telephone**, and the new information is that it was invented by **Bell**.

When the subject is not the agent (is not doing the action), then we use a passive verb.

PASSIVE

The telephone *was invented by* *Bell*.
(*The telephone* = Subject; *Bell* = Agent)

The subject (**the telephone**) is not the agent. It is the thing that the action is directed at.

2 The passive and **by the police, in 1876,** etc.

In a passive sentence, when we want to say who or what did the action, we use **by**.

On our way home we were stopped ***by the police.*** *The new hospital will be opened* ***by the premier.***
The paper was all blown away ***by the wind.***

We can give other details about the action. For example, we can use a phrase saying when or where something happens.

The telephone was invented ***in 1876.*** *The visitors will be driven* ***to the airport.***
The concerts are usually held ***at the university.***

Sometimes there is no phrase after the verb.

A new swimming pool ***is being built.*** *All the documents* ***have been destroyed.***

For more details see page 36.

Practice

A Active or passive verb? (1)

Choose the correct verb forms in this news report about a storm.

Millions of dollars' worth of damage (▶) ~~has caused~~/has been caused by a storm which (1) swept/was swept across southern Manitoba last night. The Red River (2) burst/was burst its banks after heavy rain. Many people (3) rescued/were rescued from the floods by fire-fighters, who (4) received/were received hundreds of calls for help. Wind speeds (5) reached/were reached 130 kilometres an hour in some places. Roads (6) blocked/were blocked by fallen trees, and power lines (7) brought/were brought down, leaving thousands of homes without electricity. "Everything possible (8) is doing/is being done to get things back to normal," a spokesperson (9) said/was said.

B Identifying the agent (2)

In each of these sentences underline who or what is doing the action (the agent).

▶ The traffic was all heading out of town.
1 The photo was taken by my brother.
2 The water was pouring out of the hole.
3 A cyclist has been hit by a driver.
4 We were woken up by the alarm.
5 The guide led a group of tourists through the provincial park.
6 The dog has bitten several people.

C Active and passive (1–2)

You are telling a friend some news. Use the notes to complete the second sentence. Sometimes you need to use the active and sometimes the passive.

▶ (Simple Past: Geeta/go/to Medicine Hat/last month)
You remember Geeta? She went to Medicine Hat last month.

▶ (Present Perfect: send/our luggage/to Australia)
Bad news about our luggage. It's been sent to Australia.

1 (Simple Past: Gavin Iles/win/the trivia competition)
Did you hear about the trivia competition? It ....

2 (Simple Past: Mrs. Luengo/go/skydiving/last week)
You know Mrs. Luengo? She ....

3 (Present Perfect: a bear/attack/David)
Have you heard about David? He's ....

4 (Present Progessive: build/the house)
Malcolm and Tanya have bought a house. It's still ....

5 (Simple Present: Ignacio/like/Marcie)
Did I tell you about Ignacio? He ....

6 (Present Perfect: throw away/your stamp collection)
Bad news about your stamp collection. It's ....

7 (Present Perfect: Martians/kidnap/my neighbours)
Did I mention my neighbours? They've ....

8 (Simple Past: five people/see/the ghost)
Did you hear about the ghost? It ....

Active and passive (2)

1 The passive and the agent

In a passive sentence, we sometimes mention the agent (the person or thing doing the action). We use **by** with the agent.

The cheque must be signed ***by the manager.***
The awards were presented ***by David Suzuki.***

But we mention the agent only if it is important for the meaning of the sentence. Sometimes we do not mention it.

1 We do not mention the agent if it does not add any new information.
All our money and passports were stolen.
A man was arrested last night.
We do not need to say that the money was stolen "by a thief" or that the man was arrested "by the police."

2 We do not mention the agent if it is not important.
The streets are cleaned every day.
Gold has been discovered in the Yukon.
Who discovered the gold is less important than the fact that it is there.

3 It is sometimes difficult to say who the agent is.
This kind of jacket is considered very fashionable these days.
A number of attempts have been made to find Bigfoot.

2 Empty subjects (**they**, **people**, etc.)

Compare these two sentences.

ACTIVE	PASSIVE
They *clean the streets every day.*	*The streets are cleaned every day.*

The new and important information is <u>how often</u> the streets are cleaned. We are not interested in saying who cleans them. In the active sentence we can use the "empty subject" **they**. We sometimes use a sentence with an empty subject instead of the passive, especially in conversation.

We can also use the empty subjects **people**, **you**, **one**, and **someone**.

ACTIVE	PASSIVE
People *use this bike trail all the time.*	*This bike trail is used all the time.*
You/One *should check the details.*	*The details should be checked.*
Someone *took my purse.*	*My purse was taken.*

3 When do we use the passive?

We use the passive in both speech and writing, but it is more common in writing. We see it especially in textbooks and reports. We use it to describe activities in industry, science and technology, and also for official rules.

Beef ***is exported*** *to Japan.* *The liquid* ***is heated*** *to the boiling point.*
Payment ***can be made*** *at any bank.* *Cars left here* ***will be towed*** *away.*

In these situations, it is often not important to say who is doing the action, or it is difficult to say.

The passive is also often used in news reports.

A number of political prisoners ***have been released.***
Talks ***will be held*** *in Ottawa next week.*

Practice

A The passive and the agent (1)

Milena is writing to a friend. This is part of her email.

Someone broke into our house on the weekend. The burglar took some jewellery. But luckily he didn't do any damage. A very nice young police officer interviewed me. Detectives found some fingerprints, and the police database identified the burglar. Police have arrested a man and are questioning him. But they haven't found the jewellery.

Now complete the passive sentences in this conversation. Use a phrase with *by* only if it adds information.

Milena: Our house (▶) was broken into on the weekend.
Casey: Oh no!
Milena: Some jewellery (1) .... But luckily no damage (2) ....
Casey: Did the police go to your house?
Milena: Yes, they did. I (3) ....
Casey: I don't suppose they know who did it.
Milena: Well, amazingly they do. Some (4) ...., and the (5) ....
A man (6) .... and (7) ....
Melanie: Wonderful.
Milena: There's only one problem. The (8) ....

B Active or passive sentence? (1)

Write a paragraph from the notes about the first car. Some sentences are active and some are passive. Use a phrase with *by* only if it adds information.

▶ a Belgian named Étienne Lenoir/make/ the first car	The first car was made by a Belgian named Étienne Lenoir.
1 but/Lenoir/not produce/many cars/ for sale	But Lenoir ....
2 a German called Karl Benz/start/ commercial production	Commercial ....
3 people/now/see/Benz/as the father/ of the automobile	Benz ....

C Empty subjects (2)

Reply to what people say. Use the subject in parentheses.

▶ Emmanuel: The bus fares have been increased. (they)
Sanjit: What? You mean they've increased the bus fares again!

1 Eve: Bicycles should be used for short trips. (people)
Tara: Yes, I agree. ....

2 Alex: A new source of energy has been discovered. (someone)
George: What? Did you say that ....

3 Shannon: This building is going to be torn down. (they)
Jeff: Well, no one told me that ....

4 Raj: Eggs shouldn't be kept in a freezer. (you)
Jean-Marc: Really? I didn't know ....

5 Michelle: Why isn't trash put in the garbage can? (people)
Karina: Exactly. Why don't ....

Verb + **to**-infinitive or verb + -**ing** form?

1 Introduction

Some verbs are followed by a **to**-infinitive, and some by an -**ing** form.

VERB + TO-INFINITIVE	VERB + -ING FORM
Sophie ***decided to have*** *a party.*	*Sophie* ***suggested having*** *a party.*
Decide takes a **to**-infinitive.	**Suggest** takes an -**ing** form.

A few verbs take either a **to**-infinitive or an -**ing** form.

Mika ***started to paint/started painting*** *a picture.*

2 To-infinitive or -ing form?

+ TO-INFINITIVE	+ -ING FORM
These verbs are followed by a **to**-infinitive. **agree, aim, appear, arrange, ask, attempt, beg, can't afford, can't wait** (see part 3), **choose, claim, decide, demand, desire, expect, fail, guarantee, happen** (see part 4), **help, hope, manage, offer, plan, prepare, pretend, promise, prove** (see part 4), **refuse, seem, tend, threaten, turn out** (see part 4), **undertake, want, wish**	These verbs are followed by an -**ing** form. **admit, avoid, can't face, can't help, can't resist, can't stand, carry on, consider, delay, deny, detest, dislike, enjoy, excuse, fancy, feel like, finish, give up, imagine, involve, justify, keep (on), mention, mind, postpone, practise, put off, resent, risk, save, suggest, tolerate**

3 Can't wait and feel like

If you can't wait to do something, you are eager to do it.

I ***can't wait to see*** *the photos you took.* (= I am eager/impatient to see the photos.)

If you feel like doing something, you want to do it.

Do you ***feel like going*** *out for dinner?* (= Would you like to go out for dinner?)

Feel like is informal.

4 Happen, turn out, and prove

We use **prove to** or **turn out to** when experience shows what something is like.

In the end our forecast ***proved to be*** *correct.*

Finding Nikki's house ***turned out to be*** *more difficult than Giorgio had expected.*

Note the meaning of **happen to.**

I ***happened to see*** *Rico in town.* (= I saw Rico <u>by chance</u> in town.)

5 Two forms together

We can sometimes use more than one **to**-infinitive or -**ing** form together.

The government decided ***to refuse to give*** *in to the public's demands.*

I want ***to avoid hurting*** *anyone's feelings.*

The man denied ***threatening to punch*** *a police officer.*

Practice

A To-infinitive or -ing form? (1–3)

Complete the conversation. Write a *to*-infinitive or *-ing* form.

Erdem: Are we going to take a vacation this year?
Raissa: Didn't we all decide (▶) to spend .... (spend) our vacation on a Caribbean island?
Erdem: Lovely. I enjoy (▶) lying .... (lie) on the beach.
I might manage (1) .... (get) a suntan.
Josh: I'd love a vacation. I can't wait (2) .... (leave) this place behind.
Carol: I don't feel like (3) .... (stay) in one place all the time.
I really dislike (4) .... (sit) on the beach all day.
Raissa: Well, I don't mind (5) .... (tour) around somewhere.
Carol: Erdem, you promised (6) .... (go) to Vancouver with me.
We were planning (7) .... (rent) a car.
Erdem: Vancouver? Are you sure? But I couldn't stand (8) .... (drive) all the time.
Dino: I'm afraid I can't afford (9) .... (spend) too much money.
Nigel: And I can't justify (10) .... (take) all that time off from school.

B To-infinitive or -ing form? (1–4)

Complete this article from a magazine. Write the *to*-infinitive or *-ing* form of these verbs:
accept, argue, be, ~~find~~, have, insist, lose, ~~plug~~, repair, say, take, wait

If you buy something from a store—a new stereo for example—you usually can't wait (▶) to plug ...... it in and put some music on. And of course, you expect (▶) to find .... that the equipment works. But that doesn't always happen, unfortunately. If the thing doesn't work, you should take it straight back to the store. If you delay (1) .... it back, you will risk (2) .... your rights as a customer. And you should prepare (3) .... on those rights. You may be one of those people who always avoid (4) .... with people, but in this case you should be ready for an argument. The sales clerk may prove (5) .... a true friend of the customer—it's not impossible—but first he or she will probably offer (6) .... the stereo for you. That's all right if you don't mind (7) .... a few weeks, but it isn't usually a good idea. What you should do is politely demand (8) .... your money back immediately. You may want to accept another stereo in place of the old one, but you don't have to. You should refuse (9) .... a credit note. Just keep on (10) .... that you want your money back.

C Two forms together (5)

What might you say in these situations? Write a sentence with both a *to*-infinitive and an *-ing* form.

▶ Your decision to change your vacation plans might upset Genane. You won't risk that. You don't want to. What do you say to Tomas?
I don't want to risk upsetting Genane. ....

1 You and Delia want to complain about your meal in a restaurant. You need to see the manager. Delia won't ask, but you don't mind. What do you say to her?
....

2 Mathieu doesn't like the idea of going to Scotland. But he promised. He admitted it. What do you tell Vivienne?
....

3 The band was playing. They finished just as you arrived. This was by chance. What do you tell your friends?
Just as I arrived, ...

Verb + object + to-infinitive or -ing form

1 Introduction

Customer: *None of the things I ordered have arrived. They're three weeks late. I **expect the goods to arrive** on time.*
Jean-Marc: *I'm sorry we've **kept you waiting** so long. Can I find out what the problem is and then call you back?*

Some verbs can take an object + a **to**-infinitive, and some take an object + an **-ing** form.

	VERB	OBJECT		
I	***expect***	***the goods***	***to arrive***	*on time.*
I'm sorry we've	***kept***	***you***	***waiting***	*so long.*

2 Verb + object + to-infinitive

*We **asked the doorman to let** us in.* *Jerome couldn't **persuade Rita to go** out with him.*
*The hot weather has **caused ice cream sales to increase**.*
*It **took forever to download** the pictures.*
*I didn't **mean my suggestion to be taken** seriously.*

Here are some verbs we can use in this structure: **advise, allow, ask, beg, cause, enable, encourage, expect, force, help, intend, invite, mean** (= intend), **order, recommend, remind, take** (time), **teach, tell, warn**

3 Want + object + to-infinitive

We can also use an object + a **to**-infinitive after **want**, (**would**) **like**, (**would**) **love**, (**would**) **prefer**, and (**would**) **hate.**

*Nada **wants the Flames to win**.* *We'd **hate the house to be left** empty.*

We can use this structure to give an order (see page 32).

*I **want everyone to come** here.* *I'd **like you to listen** carefully.*

We cannot normally use a **that**-clause. NOT ~~*I want that everyone comes here.*~~

4 Verb + object + -ing form

*Ramesh is so serious. I can't **imagine him having** a good time.*
*Do you **remember Julie taking** our photo?* *A new law has **stopped people texting** while driving.*

Here are some verbs we can use in this structure: **dislike, imagine, involve, keep, mind, prevent, remember, risk, stop**

5 Advise, allow, encourage, and recommend

We can use these verbs with an **-ing** form or with an object + a **to**-infinitive.

+ -ING FORM	+ OBJECT + TO-INFINITIVE
*They **allow fishing** here.*	*They **allow people to fish** here.*
*I wouldn't **recommend walking** home alone.*	*I would **advise you not to walk** home alone.*

We do not use **suggest** + an object + a **to**-infinitive.

*I **suggested** to Nick (that) he should leave.* NOT ~~*I suggested Nick to leave.*~~

Practice

A Verb + object + **to**-infinitive (2)

Report what people said. Use the verbs in parentheses.

▶ Police to motorists: Be extra cautious. (warn)
The police warned motorists to be extra cautious.

1 Guy to Roxy: Would you like to come on my talk show? (invite)
....

2 Sarah to Mark: Don't forget to get the theatre tickets. (remind)
....

3 Dentist to Deshawn: You should give up eating candy. (tell)
....

4 Police to gunman: Come out with your hands up. (order)
....

B **Would like** or **doesn't want** (3)

Complete the sentences using *would like* or *don't/doesn't want*.

▶ Carlos won't wear a tie. Sun is annoyed.
She would like him to wear a tie .... because they're going to a concert.

1 Joanne is going to go skydiving, but her son and daughter don't like the idea.
They .... because they think it's dangerous.

2 Donald is falling in love with Cristy, but she's worried about this.
She .... because she doesn't find him attractive.

3 Nina may not go on vacation with her friends.
They .... because she's always fun to be with.

C Verb + object + **to**-infinitive or **-ing** form (2, 4)

Marina Colangelo is reporting what people have said to her. She combines the two sentences into one.

▶ "The truck skidded. The icy road caused it."
The icy road caused the truck to skid.

▶ "The employees might go on strike. The company can't risk that."
The company can't risk the employees going on strike.

1 "The suspects might leave the country. The police must stop that."
....

2 "Parliament opposed him. The prime minister didn't expect that."
....

3 "The hostages lay down. The bank robbers forced them."
....

4 "The dollar is falling in value. The government doesn't mind that."
....

D **Advise, allow,** etc. (5)

Complete this paragraph from a guidebook to Toronto. Use the to-infinitive or the *-ing* form.

We wouldn't recommend (▶) driving.......... (drive) into Toronto during rush hour.
We'd advise you (1) .... (travel) by subway.
We'd recommend (2) .... (buy) a day pass, which is cheaper than paying the cash fare all day.
On weekends, the transit company allows you (3) .... (use) one pass for your whole family.
This is to encourage people (4) .... (take) public transit more on weekends and leave their cars at home.

Question word + to-infinitive

1 Introduction

Marissa uses a question word (**what**) and a **to**-infinitive (**to wear**). She is talking about the best thing to do. **I don't know what to wear** means that I don't know what I <u>should</u> wear.

2 Structures with what to do, where to go, etc.

Before the question word we can use a verb such as **ask, decide, discover, discuss, explain, find out, forget, know, learn, remember, say, think, understand, wonder.**

It was a real problem. I couldn't ***think what to do****.*
We were ***wondering where to park*** *the car.*
Carrie wants to ***know how to work*** *the computer.*
Have Jeff and Matt ***decided when to have*** *their barbecue?*

Sometimes there is a verb + object before the question word.
In this structure we can use **advise, ask, show, teach,** and **tell.**

Ava ***showed me how to change*** *a tire.*
The guide didn't ***tell the tourists when to be*** *back at the bus.*

Before the question word we can also use the adjectives **clear, obvious,** and **sure** and the expressions **have an idea** and **make up your mind.**

I wasn't ***sure who to ask*** *for help.* *Anand doesn't* ***have much idea how to cook****.*

A preposition (e.g. **of**) can come before the question word.

There's the question ***of who to invite*** *to the reception.*
You need to be informed ***about what to do*** *in an emergency.*

3 Why, what, whose, which, and whether

We cannot use **why** before a **to**-infinitive.

No one could explain ***why we had to wait.*** NOT ~~*No one could explain why to wait.*~~

After **what, which, whose, how many,** and **how much**, we can use a noun.

Gina and Marc were discussing ***what colour to paint*** *the walls.*
We wondered ***whose story to believe****—both drivers said it wasn't their fault.*
It's difficult to know ***how much luggage to take*** *with you.*

We can use **whether** but not **if** before a **to**-infinitive.

We'll have to decide ***whether to go*** *ahead with the project (or not).*
NOT ~~*We'll have to decide if to go ahead.*~~
Melanie wasn't sure ***whether to call*** *the doctor or not.*
I was wondering ***whether to order*** *some coffee.*

Practice

A Structures with **what to do, where to go**, etc. (2)

Comment on these situations.

▶ How do I turn on the computer?

1 What should I say?

2 Where shall we go?

3 How do I stop?

▶ (not know) *He doesn't know how to turn on the computer.* ....

1 (can't think) ....

2 (not sure) ....

3 (not know) ....

B Structures with **what to do, where to go**, etc. (2)

Look at the questions and then complete the paragraph about a man getting out of prison. Use a question word and a *to*-infinitive.

▶ How should he start a new life?
1 What can he expect?
2 Where should he go?
3 How can he find somewhere to live?
4 What should he do?
5 Who can he contact?

This man will have problems when he leaves prison. He needs advice on (▶) *how to start* .... a new life. After a long time in prison, he isn't sure (1) .... in the outside world and he has no idea (2) .... He doesn't know (3) .... a place to live either. But he won't be completely alone. A social worker will advise him (4) ...., so he'll know (5) .... if he needs help.

C Question word + **to**-infinitive (2–3)

You are finding it very difficult to make your mind up.
Complete your answers to the questions. Use a question word and a *to*-infinitive.

▶ Melissa: Are you going to buy that sweater?
You: I don't know *whether to buy* .... it or not.

▶ Nikhil: What time do you think we should leave?
You: I'm not really sure *what time to leave* ....

1 Nadam: Do you want to take a business course?
You: I'm wondering .... business or statistics.

2 Kajal: How much money should we spend on the present?
You: I have no idea .... on it.

3 Adil: Do you plan to join the sports club?
You: I can't decide .... it or not.

4 Chris: Which route should we take?
You: It's difficult to know ....

5 Vanessa: Which lottery numbers are you going to choose?
You: I haven't decided ....

Adjective + **to**-infinitive

1 Introduction

RACHEL IS TAKING A DRIVING LESSON.

We can use a **to**-infinitive (e.g. **to be**) after an adjective (e.g. **great**).

2 It is easy to drive the car

An adjective + **to**-infinitive often comes in this structure with **it** + **be**.

*It's **important to look** in the mirror.* *It's **lovely to see** you.*

*It's very **safe to use** the ladder.* ***It** was **silly to make** such a big deal about it.*

The subject can also be a person.

*I'm **delighted to see** you.* *We're **ready to start** now.*

3 The car is easy to drive

Compare these two sentences. They both mean the same thing.

*It is easy to drive **the car**.* ***The car** is easy to drive.*

We do not use **it** in the second sentence.

NOT ~~The car is easy to drive it~~ and NOT ~~The car it is easy to drive.~~

Here are some more examples.

*Your writing is **difficult to read**.* *A small car would be **cheap to drive**.*

*The parade was **fascinating to watch**.* *The ladder is very **safe to use**.*

We can use this structure with adjectives meaning "good" or "bad," e.g. **awful**, **bad**, **exciting**, **fascinating**, **good**, **marvellous**, **nice**, **terrible**, **wonderful**. We can also use it with these adjectives: **cheap**, **convenient**, **dangerous**, **difficult**, **easy**, **expensive**, **impossible**, **safe**, **simple**.

4 Certain, sure, and likely

We can use a **to**-infinitive after **certain**, **sure**, **likely**, and **unlikely**.

*The Canucks are **certain/sure to win**.* (= They will certainly win.)

*Editha is **likely to be** at work.* (= She is probably at work.)

5 For and of

After some adjectives we can use **for** + object + **to**-infinitive (see page 46).

*It's **important for drivers to be** careful.* *It isn't **safe for children to play** on ladders.*

After an adjective describing how someone behaves (e.g. **polite**, **silly**), we can use **of**.

*It was **polite of Sabine to write** and thank us.* (Sabine was polite.)

*It was **careless of me to forget** the tickets.* (I was careless.)

Practice

A It is easy to drive the car (2)

Sarah's job is to write advertisements. She is writing one for Compex computers. Write sentences with *it* and an adjective followed by a *to*-infinitive.

▶ Buy a Compex computer. It isn't expensive.
It isn't expensive to buy a Compex computer.

1 Using the computer is very simple.
It's very ....

2 Understanding the set-up isn't difficult.
It isn't ....

3 You can run any kind of software. It's easy.
....

4 Exploring the world of Compex is absolutely fascinating.
....

5 Try the ultimate computer experience. Are you ready?
....

B The car is easy to drive (3)

Sarah isn't happy with her ideas for the Compex ad. She is rewriting the first four sentences like this.

▶ A Compex computer isn't expensive to buy.
1 The computer ....
2 The set-up ....
3 ....
4 ....

C Certain, sure and likely (4)

Complete the conversation. Make sentences from the notes in parentheses.

Ken: Are you going to Jen and Rob's party?
Shea: Yes, I am. (▶) It's sure to be a good party (it/sure/be/a good party).
Ken: Will there be a lot of people there?
Shea: Yes, (1) .... (it/likely/be/pretty crowded).
Ken: Has Cindy been invited, do you know?
Shea: Oh, (2) .... (she/certain/be/there).
Ken: I don't know that part of town. Is the house easy to find?
Shea: No, it isn't. Take a map or (3) .... (you/unlikely/find/it).

D For and of (5)

Frank and Karla are talking about two students they know named Gary and Steve. Complete the conversation. Write *for* or *of*.

Frank: I can't believe that Gary and Steve had a fight at a bar. It was very childish (▶) of them.
Karla: Yes, it was especially stupid (1) .... them to fight about which hockey team is the best. There must be something more interesting (2) .... them to talk about.
Frank: I blame Steve. It wasn't very smart (3) .... him to knock Gary's drink over.
Karla: It was brave (4) .... Daniel to try to stop the fight. It was awful (5) .... him to get hit on the head with a chair.

For with the **to**-infinitive

1 Introduction

Bella: *I'll just call the office. The boss is waiting for me to call her back.*
John: *I don't think it was a good idea for you to bring that cellphone on vacation with you, Bella.*

We can use **for** + object + **to**-infinitive. Here are some more examples.

	FOR	OBJECT	TO-INFINITIVE
My mother has arranged	***for***	***someone***	***to look after** her dog next week.*
It's difficult	***for***	***unskilled people***	***to find** work these days.*
The crowd was impatient	***for***	***the game***	***to begin.***
It's a nuisance	***for***	***you***	***to have** to wait.*

2 For expressing purpose

We can use this structure to say why something is done (to express purpose). (See also page 104.)

*Pierre photocopied the figures **for the sales manager to have** a look at.*
(= He photocopied the figures so that the sales manager could have a look at them.)
*The store provides baskets **for the customers to put** their purchases in.*
*I'd like to put forward a few suggestions **for you to think about.***

3 Too and enough

We can use **too** and **enough** with this structure.

*The road is **too** busy **for the children to cross** safely.*
*Unfortunately the table was **too** small **for all of us to sit** around.*
*Fortunately the table was big **enough for all of us to sit** around.*
*The guide didn't speak loudly **enough for everyone to hear** clearly.*

4 For and of

FOR

We often use **for** + object + **to**-infinitive after an adjective.

*Hannah was **anxious for** the guests to arrive.*
*Would it be **possible for** you to move your car, please?*

Some of the adjectives we can use with **for**:
anxious, awful, cheap, convenient, dangerous, difficult, eager, easy, exciting, expensive, friendly, good, happy, horrible, impatient, important, interesting, necessary, nice, normal, polite, possible, ready, safe, sensible, silly, stupid, terrible, useful, willing, wonderful, wrong

OF

After an adjective saying how someone behaves, we use **of** + object + **to**-infinitive.

*It's **nice of** Tabitha to put you up for the night.*
(Tabitha is nice.)
*It was **wise of** you to call ahead.*
(You were wise.)

Some of the adjectives we can use with **of**:
brave, careless, clever, foolish, generous, good, helpful, honest, intelligent, kind, mean, nice, polite, sensible, stupid, wise, wrong

Compare these two sentences.

*It was good **for** you to come jogging.*
(= It was good for your health.)

*It was **good of** you to come jogging with me.*
(= It was a kind action by you.)

Practice

A For with the to-infinitive (1)

The second person agrees with what the first one says. Use *for* and a *to*-infinitive.

▶ Derek: Andrew should take it easy. That would be best.
Rob: Yes, you're right. It would be best for him to take it easy.

1 Shawn: Our new computer should arrive soon. I just can't wait.
Rosa: Me neither. I ....

2 Patti: Marcus shouldn't marry Raela. It would be a mistake.
Kerry: I think so too. ....

3 Customer: Advertisements should tell the truth. It's important.
Mark: I agree. ....

B For expressing purpose (2)

Write the advertisement for a vacation destination.
Match the sentence pairs and write sentences with *for* and a *to*-infinitive.

~~There are lots of activities.~~	You can enjoy them.
There's a fun pool.	You can relax in them.
There are quiet areas.	~~Guests can take part in them.~~
There are regular shows.	You can ride on it if you dare.
There's a giant roller coaster.	Children can swim in it.

▶ There are lots of activities for guests to take part in.
1 ....
2 ....
3 ....
4 ....

C Too and enough (3)

Add a sentence with *too* or *enough* and: *difficult*, ~~*funny*~~, ~~*heavy*~~, *high*, *hot*, *loud*

▶ JP and Pinder couldn't lift the piano. It was too heavy for them to lift.
▶ Michel won't repeat the joke. It isn't funny enough for him to repeat.
1 Emma can't reach the top shelf. ....
2 We can't understand the poem. ....
3 Not everyone could hear the music. ....
4 The coffee had gotten cold. Daniel couldn't drink it. ....

D For and of (4)

A Japanese company called Sanko is going to open a new factory in a small town in Saskatchewan. Write the sentences from the local newspaper.

▶ fantastic/the town/have/some new jobs
It will be fantastic for the town to have some new jobs.

▶ wise/our local council/bring/Sanko/here
It was wise of our local council to bring Sanko here.

1 difficult/the town/attract/new industry
It has been ....

2 very generous/the council/give/the land/to Sanko
It was ....

3 the company/eager/production/begin/soon
The company ....

The infinitive with and without to

This is an overview of the different structures with a **to**-infinitive (e.g. **to do**) and an infinitive without **to** (e.g. **do**).

1 The to-infinitive

We use a **to**-infinitive:

1 After an adjective (see page 44)
*It's **nice to have** a place of your own.* *The car is really **cheap to drive**.*

2 After a noun
*I must take a **book to read**.* (= a book that I <u>can</u> read)
*We've got a few **jobs to do**.* (= jobs that we <u>must</u> do)

3 With **be able to, be about to, be allowed to, be going to, have to, ought to** and **used to**
*We **aren't allowed to** park here.* *The game **is about to start**.*
*We**'re going to buy** a TV.* *You **have to fill** in a form.*

4 After some verbs, e.g. **decide, hope, manage, offer**
*Jay **decided to leave** early.* ***I hope to see** you soon.*
*Did you **manage to sort** out the problem?* *Henri **offered to pay** for the meal.*

5 After some verbs + object (see page 40)
*Martha **convinced Alex to put** up some shelves.*
*I **want you to do** something for me.*

6 After **for** + object (see page 46)
*We've arranged **for you to visit** our head office.*
*It is important **for students to register** with the student services office.*

7 After a question word (see page 42)
*We don't know **where to leave** our coats.*
*This book tells you **how to train** sled dogs.*

8 To say why (see page 104)
*Raul went out **to play** golf.* *I need the money **to pay** the phone bill.*

2 The infinitive without to

We use an infinitive without **to**:

1 After **can, could, may, might, must, needn't, shall, should, will,** and **would**
*We **could go** to a club.* *I **must speak** to the manager.*
*It **might snow** later.* *Adelfina **will be** away for three days.*

2 After **had better** and **would rather**
*It's cold. You**'d better wear** a coat.* ***I'd rather listen** to Sarah McLachlan than Nickelback.*

3 After **make** + object and **let** + object
*That show was funny. It really **made me laugh**.*
*Curtis will be here at five. His boss is going to **let him leave** work early.*

4 After **see** or **hear** + an object (see page 52)
*They **saw the lights come** on.* *We all **heard the band play**.*

3 Help

An infinitive after **help** can be with or without **to**.
*Can I **help (to) get** dessert?* *Jermaine **helped** me **(to) choose** a present.*

Practice

A The to-infinitive (1)

Comment on these situations. Join each pair of sentences using a *to*-infinitive.

► Kerwood will give you a lift. He promised.
You: Kerwood ...promised to give me a lift....

1 You want to eat. You must have something.
You: I must ....

2 You are taking a break. It's nice.
You: It's ....

3 Will Connie speak to Evan? He wants her to.
Evan ....

4 Hiroshi can't fix the TV. He doesn't know how to.
....

5 Ling and her sister are going to Mexico. They have decided.
....

6 Morgan is visiting James. She has gone to the hospital.
....

7 Sasha is doing some studying. Unfortunately she has to.
....

8 Bida must call the office. It's important.
....

B The infinitive without to (2)

Write the missing verbs. Usually more than one answer is correct.

► I've been fixing the car. I really must ...wash... my hands.
1 What's in the email? Why won't you let me .... it?
2 Did you see that beautiful old car .... past a moment ago?
3 It was a very sad story. It made me ....
4 I don't want to do anything active. I'd rather .... on the beach.
5 It's very cold. I think it might .... for the first time this winter.
6 I keep getting this pain in my leg. I think I'd better .... a doctor.

C The infinitive with and without to (1–2)

Luc and Lydia are at the train station. Lydia is going away for the weekend.
Write the infinitive of the verbs. You have to decide whether or not you need *to*.

Luc: Are you sure you'll (►) ...be... (be) all right?
Lydia: Yes, of course. I'm not a child. I can manage (►) ...to look... (look) after myself.
Luc: OK, sorry.
Lydia: Some friends have invited me (1) .... (visit) them. I'm not going to the North Pole.
Luc: It'll be nice for you (2) .... (see) your old friends again. I just know you're going (3) .... (have) lots of fun. Let me (4) .... (buy) you a magazine (5) .... (read) on the train.
Lydia: I can't (6) .... (read) when I'm travelling. It makes me (7) .... (feel) sick, even in a train. I'd rather just (8) .... (look) out of the window.
Luc: OK. Well, you'd better (9) .... (get) on. I think it's about (10) .... (leave). Oh, did I remind you (11) .... (transfer) at Ottawa?
Lydia: Yes, Luc, you did. Don't worry, I won't (12) .... (forget). I know perfectly well how (13) .... (get) there.

Afraid to do or afraid of doing?

1 Afraid

*Roberto is **afraid to climb** the ladder.*
(= He doesn't want to climb the ladder because he is afraid.)

*Roberto is **afraid of falling.***
(= He is afraid because he might fall.)

Here are some more examples.

*I was **afraid to say** anything in front of all those people.*
*Jun Jun was **afraid to wander** too far from the hotel.*

*I was **afraid of sounding** foolish, you see.*
*She was **afraid of getting** lost.*

2 Anxious, ashamed, and interested

Compare these examples.

*The company is **anxious to increase** their sales.*
(= They want to increase their sales.)

*Ivan was **anxious about presenting** his report.*
(= He was worried because he had to present his report.)

*I'm **ashamed to tell you** what I scored on the test.*
(= I don't want to tell you because I'm ashamed.)

*I'm **ashamed of getting** such a low score.*
(= I'm ashamed because I got such a low score.)

*I'd be **interested to meet** Brianne.*
(= I want to meet her.)

*Brianne is **interested in painting**.*
(= It is an interest/a hobby of hers.)

*I was **interested to hear** Miguel's story.*
(= I found his story interesting.)

3 Structures with sorry

To apologize for something we are doing, we use a **to**-infinitive.

*I'm **sorry to tell** you this, but your test score is pretty low.*
*I'm **sorry to call** so late, but it's important.*

To express regret, we also use a **to**-infinitive.

*I was **sorry to hear** that Arvid's uncle had died.*

To apologize for something we did, we can use **about** + **-ing** form.

*I'm **sorry about making** all that noise last night.*
(OR *I'm **sorry I made** all that noise last night.*)

Practice

A Afraid (1)

Complete the sentences. Use these words and put the verb into the *to*-infinitive or *-ing* form:
~~dive into the water~~, drop them, fall, move

▶ 

1 

2 

3 

▶ He's afraid to dive into the water.

1 She's afraid ....

2 She's afraid ....

3 He's afraid ....

B Afraid (1)

Read what people say and write a comment about each person.
Rewrite the second sentence using *afraid to* or *afraid of*.

▶ Greta: There's a large bull in the field. I don't want to open the gate.
Greta is afraid to open the gate.

▶ Ryan: I arrived at the airport on time. I thought I might get stuck in traffic.
Ryan was afraid of getting stuck in traffic.

1 Effem: I was going to go bungee jumping yesterday. But I couldn't jump.
....

2 Olga: The policeman looked angry. I didn't want to argue with him.
....

3 Maurice: I'm keeping my shirt on. I might get sunburnt.
....

C Afraid, anxious, ashamed, and interested (1–2)

Complete the conversation. Write a *to*-infinitive or a preposition + *-ing* form.

Sian: I'm ashamed (▶) to admit (admit) it, but airplanes terrify me. I get really anxious (▶) about flying (fly). I'm afraid (1) .... (buy) a plane ticket. I can't stand being on a plane. I'm afraid (2) .... (get) killed. I feel ashamed (3) .... (be) so scared.

Sarah: Aren't there things you can do to overcome your fear?

Sian: Well, I was interested (4) .... (read) in the paper recently that you can take a course that helps you. I'm anxious (5) .... (reserve) a place in the course very soon.

D Sorry (3)

Complete the conversation. Use a *to*-infinitive or *about* + *-ing* form. Look at the information in parentheses.

Peter: I'm sorry (▶) to disturb you (I'm disturbing you), but could I just say something? I'm sorry (1) .... (I was so rude) last night. I didn't mean what I said.

Francine: Oh, that's OK. I'm sorry (2) .... (I lost my temper).

Peter: Right. OK. And, as I said, sorry (3) .... (I'm interrupting you).

See it happen or see it happening?

1 Introduction

Sotiris fell down the stairs.
*Mira **saw him fall**.*

Sotiris was walking with a cane.
*Mira **saw him walking** across the road.*

2 See it happen

After some verbs we can use an object + an infinitive without to.

	VERB	OBJECT	INFINITIVE	
Mira	***saw***	***Sotiris***	***fall***	*down the stairs.*
Anil	***heard***	***someone***	***close***	*the door.*
Let's	***watch***	***the parade***	***go***	*past.*
We all	***felt***	***the house***	***shake.***	

We can use this structure with these verbs: **feel, hear, listen to, notice, see, watch**

3 See it happening

We can also use an **-ing** form after the object.

	VERB	OBJECT	-ING FORM	
Mira	***saw***	***Sotiris***	***walking***	*with a cane.*
Can you	***hear***	***someone***	***playing***	*the piano?*
We	***found***	***Matthew***	***exercising***	*in the gym.*
I could	***feel***	***an insect***	***crawling***	*up my leg.*

We can use this structure with these verbs: **feel, find, hear, listen to, notice, see, smell, watch**

4 See it happen or see it happening?

SEE IT HAPPEN

*We saw Zack **plant** the tree.*
(He planted the tree. We saw him do the whole job.)
*I watched Nick **light** a cigarette.*
*We noticed a young man **sit** down and order a meal.*

SEE IT HAPPENING

*We saw Zack **planting** the tree.*
(He was planting the tree. We saw him in the middle of the job.)
*I watched Nick **smoking** a cigarette.*
*We noticed a young man **sitting** at the table eating a meal.*

When we talk about a short action, it often does not matter which structure we use.

*They heard a car **turn/turning** the corner.* *I didn't see anyone **leave/leaving** any litter.*

Practice

A See it happen (2)

Rene is in court. He is answering questions about Mr. Lewis, who the police suspect of a number of crimes. Add a sentence using the verb in parentheses.

▶ And you say a second man came into the restaurant? (see)
Rene: That's right. I saw him come in.

1 Are you certain that Mr. Lewis took the envelope? (see)
Rene: Yes, absolutely. ……………………………

2 Then Mr. Lewis left the restaurant, did he? (watch)
Rene: He left soon afterwards. ……………………………

3 And he drove away. (hear)
Rene: Yes, he did. ……………………………

B See it happening (3)

Look at the pictures and add a sentence with *I can see/hear/smell ...* and the *-ing* form of these verbs: *bark*, *burn*, ~~*come*~~, *ring*, *wave*

▶ 
1 
2 
3 
4 

▶ The mail carrier is on his way. I can see him coming.
1 There's a phone upstairs. ……………………………
2 There's a woman in the boat. ……………………………
3 There are some dogs outside. ……………………………
4 You've forgotten your lunch. ……………………………

C See it happen or see it happening? (4)

There has been a gas explosion downtown. TV reporter Sarita Swain is asking people about it. What did people see or hear?

▶ Man: The gas line exploded. I heard it. It was a shock.
He heard the gas line explode.

▶ Woman: A man was lying in the road. I saw him. He was just lying there.
She saw a man lying in the road.

1 Woman: The building shook. I felt it. I couldn't believe it.
……………………………

2 Man: People were shouting. I heard them. There was panic.
……………………………

3 Girl: An alarm was ringing. I could hear it. It went on and on.
……………………………

4 Boys: The police arrived. We saw them. They were over there.
……………………………

5 Man: I saw a woman. She was crying. She was very upset.
……………………………

Agreement

1 Subject and verb

Look at these examples of agreement between the subject (e.g. **the window**) and the verb (e.g. **is**).

SINGULAR	PLURAL
*The **window is** open.*	*The **windows are** open.*
***She was** upset.*	*The door **and** the window **are** open.*
***It has** been raining.*	*Her **eyes were** wet.*
*The **soup tastes** good.*	***They have** a new puppy.*
*This method **doesn't work**.*	*The **cookies taste** good.*
	*These **methods don't** work.*
After a singular or an uncountable noun and after **he**, **she**, or **it**, we use a singular verb.	After a plural noun or **they**, and after nouns joined by **and**, we use a plural verb.

2 Everyone, something, every, all, etc.

After **everyone, something, nothing**, etc, we use a singular verb (see also page 68).

***Everyone was** pleased.* ***Something is** wrong.*

But compare these examples with **every**, **each**, and **all**.

After a phrase with **every** or **each**, we use a singular verb.	After **all** and a plural noun, we use a plural verb.
***Every seat has** a number.* ***Each door is** a different colour.*	***All the seats have** numbers.*

3 One of, a number of, and a lot of

After **one of ...**, we use a singular verb.	After **a number of ...**, we normally use a plural verb.
***One** of the photos **is** missing.*	***A number of** questions **were** asked.*

After **a lot of ...**, the verb agrees with the noun.

*Every year a lot of **pollution is** created, and a lot of **trees are** cut down.*

4 Any of, either of, neither of, and none of

When a plural noun comes after **any of, either of, neither of**, or **none of**, a singular verb should be used for agreement. In spoken English, however, we usually use a plural verb.

***Is/Are any** of these old maps worth keeping?*
*I wonder if **either** of those alternatives **is/are** a good idea.*
***Neither** of these cameras **works/work** properly.*
***None** of the plants **has/have** grown very much.*

5 An amount + a singular verb

After an amount of money, a distance, a weight, or a length of time, we normally use a singular verb.

***Eight dollars seems** like a fair price.* ***A hundred metres isn't** far to swim.*
***Ninety kilograms is** too heavy for me to lift.* ***Five minutes doesn't** seem long to wait.*

We are talking about the amount as a whole, not the individual dollars or metres.

Practice

A Subject and verb (1)

Scott and Sandy are in an antique shop. Complete the conversation by choosing the correct form of the verb.

Scott: This table (▶) is/~~are~~ lovely.
Sandy: Yes, the wood (1) is/are beautiful, isn't it?
Scott: The style and the colour (2) is/are both perfect for what we want.
Sandy: These chairs (3) looks/look very stylish, too, but they (4) is/are very expensive.
Scott: Can you see if the table (5) has/have got a price on it?
Sandy: Yes, it has. It says it (6) costs/cost $2000. That's ridiculous.
Scott: Don't you think prices (7) has/have gone up recently? Those tables we saw last month (8) wasn't/weren't so expensive.

B **Everyone, every,** etc., and phrases with **of** (2–4)

Jaclyn has been to a very fancy party. She is telling her parents about it. Write *was* or *were*.

I really enjoyed the party. It (▶) ..was.... wonderful. Each guest (1) .... welcomed by the hostess in person. All the rooms (2) .... crowded with people. Everyone (3) .... enjoying themselves. A lot of people (4) .... dancing, and a number of people (5) .... swimming in the pool out back. All the people there (6) .... very impressive. One of the guests (7) .... a TV personality—the talk-show host Marcel Beaudin. I didn't know many of the guests. None of my friends (8) .... there.

C Agreement (1–4)

Jean-Claude is making a documentary about police work. A police officer is talking about her job. Choose the correct form.

▶ Every police officer is/~~are~~ given special training for the job.
1 No two days are the same. Each day is/are different.
2 But the job isn't/aren't as exciting or glamorous as some people think.
3 Not all police officers is/are allowed to carry guns.
4 A number of police officers here works/work with dogs.
5 An officer and her dog has/have to work closely together.
6 One of our jobs is/are to prevent crime from happening in the first place.
7 A lot of crime is/are caused by people being careless.
8 Sorry, I have to go now. Someone has/have just reported a robbery.

D An amount + a singular verb (5)

Combine the questions and answers about travel and holidays into one sentence using *is* or *are*.

▶ Do you know the price of a room? ~ One hundred dollars.
One hundred dollars is the price of a room.
▶ How many national statutory holidays are there? ~ Five days each year.
Five days each year are national statutory holidays.
1 Are you going on a long walk? ~ Fifteen kilometres.
....
2 Who's travelling on the bus? ~ Eight students.
....
3 Was someone waiting for the museum to open? ~ Yes, three people.
....
4 Do you know the baggage allowance? ~ Twenty kilograms.
....

A/an and the

1 Introduction

We use **a/an** when we aren't saying which one, and we use **the** when we know which one.

*A **tourist** arrived in Victoria to look around **the city**.*

2 The sun, etc.

When there is only one of the things we are talking about, we use **the**.

***The sun** was going down.* ***The government** is unpopular.*

*A drive in **the country** would be nice.* *We shouldn't pollute **the environment**.*

Normally there is only one sun or one government in the context.
We mean the government of our country and the sun in our solar system.

We normally say: **the country(side), the earth, the environment, the government, the moon, the ozone layer, the prime minister, the sky, the sun, the weather**

We also use **the** with **theatre** and **(news)paper**.

*Do you often go to **the theatre**?* *I read about the accident in **the paper**.*

Note that we say **a/the police officer** but **the police**.

***A police officer** came to the hotel.* NOT ~~*A police came to the hotel.*~~

***The police** came to the hotel.* (= one or more police officers)

3 A nice day, etc.

A phrase which describes something has **a/an.**

*It was **a lovely day**.* *Victoria is **a scenic city**.*

*It's **a big hotel**.* *This is **a better photo**.*

But we use **the** with a superlative.

*It's **the biggest hotel** in town.* *This is **the best photo**.*

We also use **a/an** to classify something—to say what kind of thing it is.

*The play was **a comedy**.* *The man's disappearance was **a mystery**.*

We use **a/an** to say what someone's job is.

*My brother is **a receptionist**.* *Carlos is **a car salesman**.*

4 A or an?

The choice of **a** or **an** and the pronunciation of **the** depend on the next sound.

a /ə/ or *the* /ðə/ + consonant sound			*an* /ən/ or *the* /ði/ + vowel sound		
***a** cup*	/k/	***the** /ðə/ cup*	***an** atlas*	/æ/	***the** /ði/ atlas*
***a** poster*	/p/	***the** /ðə/ poster*	***an** egg*	/e/	***the** /ði/ egg*
***a** ship*	/ʃ/	etc.	***an** igloo*	/ɪ/	etc.
***a** birch tree*	/b/		***an** old photo*	/əʊ/	
***a** ring*	/r/		***an** umbrella*	/ʌ/	

It is the sound of the next word that matters, not the spelling.

***a** one-way street*	/w/	***an** open door*	/əʊ/
***a** uniform*	/j/	***an** uncle*	/ʌ/
***a** holiday*	/h/	***an** hour*	/aʊ/
***a** U-turn*	/j/	***an** MP*	/e/

Practice

A The sun, etc. (1–2)

Complete these sentences about pollution and the environment. Write *a*, *an*, or *the*.

▶ There was ..a...... show on TV about dangers to ..the... environment.
1 There was also .... article in .... paper about pollution.
2 .... ozone layer will continue to disappear if we don't find .... way to stop this.
3 .... world's weather is changing. Pollution is having .... effect on our climate.
4 Last week .... oil tanker spilled oil into .... ocean, damaging wildlife.
5 Some professors have signed .... letter of protest and have sent it to .... government.
6 If .... earth was .... human being, it would be in the hospital.

B The use of a/an and the (1–3)

Complete the conversations. Write *a*, *an*, or *the*.

▶ Evelyn: How was your trip to ..the..... beach?
Paul: Wonderful. .The..... sun shone all day. We had ..a....... great time.
1 Karim: Would you like .... cigarette?
Kara: No, thanks. I've given up smoking. It's .... bad habit.
2 Janna: What's your brother doing now? Does he have .... good job?
Sally: Yes, he's .... teacher. He works at .... local high school. He loves it. It's .... great life, he says.
3 Bruce: I went to see Doctor Pascoe yesterday. She's .... best doctor I've ever had.
Tina: She's very nice, isn't she? You couldn't meet .... nicer person.
4 Rachel: You were at .... grocery store .... long time.
Kristina: Yes, I know. There was .... enormous lineup. I was thinking of complaining to .... manager.
5 Kevin: Why were you late for your meeting?
Phil: Well, first I had to go to .... hotel where I'm staying. I took .... taxi from .... airport, and .... driver got completely lost. It was .... real hassle. .... man was .... complete idiot.
6 Katie: Is this .... book you were telling me about?
Lance: Yes, it's .... really interesting story.
Katie: What did you say it's about?
Lance: I knew you weren't listening to me. It's .... science fiction story. It's about .... beginning of .... universe.

C A or an? (4)

Write the abbreviations with *a* or *an*.

▶ a personal assistant	a PA
▶ a Royal Canadian Mounted Police officer	an RCMP officer
1 a disc jockey	....
2 a very important person	....
3 an Ontario Provincial Police officer	....
4 a personal computer	....
5 a Los Angeles suburb	....
6 an unidentified flying object	....
7 an annual general meeting	....
8 a Member of Parliament	....

A/an, one, and some

1 A/an and some

Look at this example.

Will has found ***some money*** *in his old pants.*
There's ***a bill*** *and* ***some coins.***

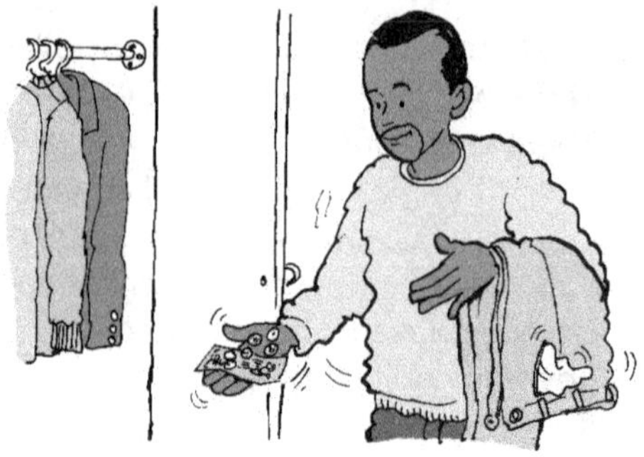

We use **a/an** with a singular noun and **some** with a plural or an uncountable noun (see part 4).

A + singular noun:	**a bill**
Some + plural noun:	**some coins**
Some + uncountable noun:	**some money**

2 A/an and one

A/an and **one** both refer to one thing. Using **one** puts more emphasis on the number.

Kevin gave the taxi driver ***a bill.*** (not a coin)
Kevin gave the taxi driver ***one bill.*** (not two)

We use **one** (not **a/an**) when we mean one of a larger number.

One question/One of the questions on the test *was more difficult than the others.*
The team wasn't at full strength. ***One player/One of the players*** *was injured.*

3 A dog = all dogs

We often use a plural noun on its own to express a general meaning (see page 60).

Dogs *make wonderful pets.* ***Oranges*** *contain vitamin C.*

Here **dogs** means "all dogs, dogs in general."

These sentences with **a/an** express the same general meaning.

A dog *makes a wonderful pet.* ***An orange*** *contains vitamin C.*
A butcher *is someone who sells meat.* ***A kitten*** *is a baby cat.*

A dog here is less common than the structure with **dogs**, but we often use **a/an** when explaining the meaning of a word, e.g. **a butcher**.

4 Some

Some with a plural noun means "a number of," and **some** with an uncountable noun means "an amount of."

Brenda took ***some photos.*** *We went out with* ***some friends.***
George bought ***some flowers.*** *I had* ***some fries*** *with my steak.*
Can you lend me ***some money?*** *Hong is doing* ***some work.***
Let's play ***some music.*** *There's* ***some milk*** *in the fridge.*

Brenda took some photos means that she took a number of photos, although we may not know the exact number.

We do not use **some** when we are describing something or saying what kind of thing it is.

Reika has ***blue eyes.*** *Is this* ***salt*** *or* ***sugar?***
These are ***fantastic photos.*** *Those people are* ***tourists.***

Compare these sentences.

I had ***some fries*** *with my steak.* (a number of fries)
I had ***fries*** *with my steak.* (fries, not mashed potatoes or rice)

Practice

A A/an and some (1)

Paul has painted some pictures for an exhibit. Describe what is in the pictures. Use *a* or *some* with these words: *birds*, *cat*, ~~*fish*~~, *flowers*, *fruit*, *luggage*, ~~*people*~~

▶ some people
▶ a fish
1 ....
2 ....
3 ....
4 ....
5 ....

▶

▶

1

2

3

4

5

B A/an and one (2)

Write *a*, *an*, or *one*.

▶ Do you only have ..one.......... bedroom? I thought you had two.
1 Nadia wanted something to drink. She was looking for .... café.
2 It was Sunday. .... store was open, but all the others were closed.
3 .... of these photos is of you. Would you like it?
4 Shall I take .... photo of you two together?

C A dog = all dogs (3)

Match each word with the correct description and write sentences with *a/an*.

~~carrot~~	small boat	▶	A carrot is a vegetable.
violin	book of maps	1	....
kayak	~~vegetable~~	2	....
atlas	tool for digging	3	....
spade	musical instrument	4	....

D Some (4)

What would you say in these situations? Use a noun and decide if you need *some* or not.

▶ You and your friend would like to play cards, but neither of you has a deck.
We need some cards.
▶ You are describing Rachel to someone. Rachel's hair is dark.
Rachel has dark hair.
1 You are eating nuts. Offer them to your friend.
Would you like ....?
2 You want a drink of water. There's a pitcher on the table, but you don't know what's in it.
Is there .... in this pitcher?
3 You've come home from a shopping trip with a few shirts and dresses. Tell your friend.
I've bought ....
4 You are eating some bread that Maria baked. It's delicious.
Maria, this is ....
5 The two women who live next door to you are both studying at the university.
Tell your visitor. The women next door are ....

Cars or the cars?

1 Introduction

We can use a plural noun (e.g. **cars, parties**) or an uncountable noun (e.g. **hockey, music**) without **the.** *I love parties* means that I love all parties, parties in general.

2 General and specific meanings

GENERAL

A plural noun or an uncountable noun on its own has a general meaning.

__Cars__ are expensive to buy.
__Elephants__ are intelligent animals.
I don't understand __computers__.
(= all computers, computers in general)
You always need __money__.
__Glass__ is made from sand.
I like __curry__.
Steve is studying __music__.
(= all music, music in general)

SPECIFIC

The + plural noun or uncountable noun has a specific meaning.

__The cars__ had both broken down.
We saw __the elephants__ at the zoo.
__The computers__ crashed at work today.
(= the specific computers at my workplace)
Larissa put __the money__ in her purse.
David swept up __the__ broken __glass__.
__The curry__ was delicious, thank you.
__The music__ was too loud. (= the music at a specific time—at a party, for example)

A phrase or clause after the noun often shows that it is specific.

Look at __the oil on your sweater__. *__The apples you gave me__ were tasty.*

But the nouns in these sentences have a general meaning.

I hate __people who never say hello__. *__Life in the old days__ was hard.*

Life in the old days is still a general idea, not a specific life.

A phrase with **of** usually takes **the.** Compare these two structures.

a book on __Aboriginal history__ *a book on __the history of Aboriginals__*

3 Special uses of the

We use **the** + singular noun to make general statements about animals and about inventions and discoveries.

__The tiger__ can swim. *__The fly__ is a common insect.*
Who invented __the camera__? *__The electron__ is a part of every atom.*

Here **the tiger** means all tigers, tigers in general. We use this structure mainly in written English. In speech, *Tigers can swim* is more common.

We also use **the** with musical instruments.

Steve can play __the piano__, __the violin__, and __the clarinet__.

We do not use **the** with sports.

Shall we play __tennis__? NOT ~~*Shall we play the tennis?*~~

Note that we *listen to the radio* but normally *watch television.*

Practice

A He likes golf (1)

Look at the pictures and describe what people like. Use these objects: *art*, *chemistry*, *fries*, *dogs*, ~~*golf*~~

▶ He likes golf.

1 ....

2 ....

3 ....

4 ....

B General and specific meanings (2)

Complete the conversations. Write the nouns and decide if you need *the*.

▶ Jake: Did you see the football (football) game on TV last night?
Liem: No, I hate football (football). I was watching the news (news) instead.

1 Dean: Did your family have a dog when you were younger?
Eric: No, thank goodness. I'm afraid of .... (dogs). I didn't like .... (dogs) that were running around in the park yesterday. I was afraid they were going to attack me.

2 Melanie: You shouldn't drive so much, Martin. You know that .... (cars) cause .... (pollution), don't you?
Martin: Yes, but .... (cars) these days are cleaner than they used to be. Isn't it .... (airplanes) that are mainly responsible for .... (pollution) of the atmosphere?

3 Teri: I put some bread out in the yard for .... (birds).
Tom: You like .... (birds), don't you?
Teri: Yes, I do. I love .... (wildlife), in fact. I'd much rather live in the country if I could.

4 Janice: You're always reading books about .... (history), aren't you?
Shirley: It was always my favourite subject. Do you know anything about .... (history) of this area?
Janice: No, but if you like going to .... (museums) and .... (old buildings), we could find out about it together.

C Special uses of the (3)

Write the correct noun and decide if you need *the*.
Use these nouns: *atom*, *rugby*, *guitar*, ~~*radio*~~, *telescope*, *television*

▶ I was listening to a call-in show on the radio .

1 Rutherford split .... in 1911.

2 Jimmy and his friends played .... in the park.

3 Casey is very musical. He can play ....

4 The children spend a lot of time watching ....

5 Galileo developed .... for use in astronomy.

On Friday, for lunch, etc.

1 Introduction

Hector: *Don't forget we're meeting on* ***Friday*** *for* ***lunch.***
Robin: *Of course I haven't forgotten. But remind me where we're eating.*
Hector: *The Riverside Restaurant. You've been there before. Claire was with us. It was* ***the Friday*** *before she went to Australia. We had* ***a*** *good* ***lunch.***

Phrases of time are usually without **a/an** or **the.**

We're meeting on ***Friday*** *for* ***lunch.***

But we use **a/an** or **the** if there is a phrase or clause after **Friday, lunch,** etc.

It was ***the Friday*** *before she went to Australia.*

We normally use **a/an** or **the** if there is an adjective.

We had ***a*** *good* ***lunch.***

2 Years, seasons, and months

I was born in ***1994.***
We play soccer ***in summer/in the summer.***
Winter *always depresses me.*
I start the course in ***September.***

That was ***the year*** *I was born.*
It was ***the winter*** *of 2007 when things started to go wrong for the company.*

3 Special times

We go away at ***Christmas (time).***
Ramadan *is early this year.*
I'll be home for ***Rosh Hashanah.***

We had ***a*** *wonderful* ***Christmas.***
We first met ***the Ramadan*** *before last.*

4 Days of the week

Yes, ***Thursday*** *will be convenient.*
I'll see you on ***Tuesday*** *evening.*

The storm was on ***the Thursday*** *of that week.*
We went canoeing on ***the weekend.***

5 Parts of the day and night

I can't sleep at ***night.***
I prefer to travel at ***night.***
I must get to bed before ***midnight.***

It's warmer in/during ***the day.***
I prefer to travel during ***the day.***
Someone got up in/during ***the night.***
We're meeting in ***the morning.***
They arrived at the hotel in ***the evening.***

We were on the beach at ***sunset.***
I hope to get there before ***dark.***

It was ***a*** *beautiful* ***sunset.***
I couldn't see in ***the dark.***

6 Meals

I'll see you at ***breakfast.***
We have ***dinner*** *at about eight.*
I'm going out after ***lunch.***

We had ***a*** *quick* ***breakfast.***
The dinner *Dave made was excellent.*
The meal *was very nice.*
We'll need ***a small meal.***

Practice

A On Friday, etc. (2–5)

Complete the conversations. Write the words and use *a*, *an*, or *the* if you need to.

▶ Rachel: Is it the music festival on Friday............ (Friday)?
Vicky: I think it's the Friday...... (Friday) after that.

1 Henry: Will you be in town for .... (Thanksgiving)?
Claire: Oh no. That's in .... (October), isn't it?

2 Nick: Are you doing anything on .... (weekend)?
Tom: Well, I'm going to the game on .... (Saturday), of course.

3 Ilona: Does it snow here at .... (Christmas)?
Emma Not often. We haven't had .... (white Christmas) for years.

4 Nick: How long have you lived here?
Harriet: We came here in .... (summer) of .... (2008).

5 Laura: I'd like to look around the lighthouse in .... (afternoon).
Trevor: Well, it's just a ruin. The building dates from .... (year) 1800.

6 Mark: I like driving at .... (night) when the roads are quiet.
Trevor: Oh, I don't like driving in .... (dark). I'd much rather travel during .... (day).

B A/an or the with meals (6)

Leslie is talking about the food she and Bryan had on vacation.
Write the words and use *a*, *an*, or *the* if you need to.

(▶) The meals...................... (meals) we had weren't very good. We had (1) .... (breakfast) in the hotel, and that wasn't too bad. We usually went out for (2) .... (lunch) because (3) .... (lunch) they served in the hotel was always the same. And (4) .... (dinner) we had at the hotel on our first day was pretty awful, so we tried a few restaurants. On our last day, we had (5) ....(fantastic meal) in a Chinese restaurant. I wish we'd discovered the place a bit sooner.

C On Friday, for lunch, etc. (1–6)

Write the words. Decide if you need to use *the*.

Shari: Hello, Khalid. Come in.
Khalid: Oh, sorry. You're having (▶) lunch............... (lunch).
Shari: No, this is (1) .... (breakfast). I had a late night. It was way after (2) .... (midnight) when I got home.
Khalid: Someone told me you're going away after (3) .... (Christmas).
Shari: Yes, I'm going to Cuba on (4) .... (Wednesday).
Khalid: What a life you lead, Shari. What time do you leave for the airport?
Shari: Oh, in (5) .... (morning) some time. About ten. It's cheaper to fly at (6) .... (night), but I decided it would be easier during (7) .... (day).
Khalid: I can drive you to the airport. I'm usually free on (8) .... (Wednesday) mornings. I'd like to see you off.
Shari: That's sweet of you Khalid, but I can take a taxi.
Khalid: I'll just check in my schedule that it isn't (9) .... (Wednesday) of our next board meeting. No, it's OK. I can do it. And when will you be back?
Shari: At the beginning of (10) .... (February). The second, I think.

The possessive form and of

1 Form

We use the possessive of a noun in phrases like *the boy's name* and *Mickey's room*.
We form the possessive like this.

Singular noun:	's	*boy* → *boy's*	*Mickey* → *Mickey's*
Plural noun ending in s:	'	*boys* → *boys'*	*tourists* → *tourists'*
Plural noun not ending in s:	's	*men* → *men's*	*children* → *children's*

We can use the possessive form with another noun or on its own.
*I've met **Angie's family**, but I haven't met **Jonathan's**.* (*Jonathan's* = Jonathan's family)

2 The boy's name or the name of the boy?

Compare these structures.

THE POSSESSIVE FORM	PHRASE WITH OF
*the **boy's** name*	*the name **of the boy***
*the **boys'** names*	*the names **of the boys***
*the **men's** names*	*the names **of the men***

Sometimes we can use either the possessive (*the boy's name*) or a phrase with **of** (*the name of the boy*), but often only one is possible. We normally use the possessive with people and animals.
***my friend's** house* ***Ava's** idea* ***Daniel's** brother* ***our neighbour's** garden* ***the dog's** owner*
***the policemen's** uniforms* ***the women's** changing room* ***the Parkers'** car*

We normally use **of** with things, and not the possessive form.
*the side **of the house*** NOT ~~*the house's side*~~
*the result **of the game*** NOT ~~*the game's result*~~
*the day **of the meeting*** NOT ~~*the meeting's day*~~

But we use **of** with people when there is a long phrase.
*the house **of one of our teachers at college***
*the address **of those people we met in Mexico***
NOT ~~*those people who we met in Mexico's address*~~

We can use both structures for places and organizations.
Vancouver's** museums* OR *the museums **of Vancouver
the earth's** atmosphere* OR *the atmosphere **of the earth
the company's** future* OR *the future **of the company
the government's** intentions* OR *the intentions **of the government

3 The possessive of time

We can use the possessive to say "when" or "how long."
***last week's** concert* ***today's** TV shows* ***yesterday's** news*
*about **a month's** work* ***a moment's** silence*

Note also:
*in **two months'** time* (two months from now)
***a week's** wages* (wages for a week)

Practice

A The possessive form (1)

Write descriptions of the things in the photos. Use *boy*, *girl*, and *children* and these words: *bike*, *cat*, ~~*dog*~~, *skateboards*, *tent*, *trophies*

▶ 
1 
2 
3 
4 
5 

▶ the children's dog........
1 ....
2 ....
3 ....
4 ....
5 ....

B The possessive form (1)

Kris is showing Jamie her photos. Write the possessive form of the nouns.

Kris: This was taken in (▶) my friend's........ (my friend) backyard.
It was (1) .... (the twins) birthday party.
This is Kerry, (2) .... (Luke) girlfriend.
And that's (3) .... (Jason) sister Emily.

Jamie: And who are these two?

Kris: That's (4) .... (Nicola) mother.
She's talking to Monica Tseng, (5) .... (her children) teacher.
And that's (6) .... (the Polewskis) dog sitting on
(7) .... (Olivia) foot.

C The boy's name or the name of the boy? (2)

Jean Menard writes detective stories. Here are the titles of some of his stories. Write the titles using either *of* or a possessive form (with *'s* or *s'*).

▶ the mistake/the policeman — The Policeman's Mistake........
▶ the bottom/the bottle — The Bottom of the Bottle........
1 the gun/Mr. Malveaux ....
2 the smell/blood ....
3 the car/the killer ....
4 the middle/the night ....
5 the death/someone important ....
6 the money/the gangsters ....

D The possessive of time (3)

Rewrite the underlined phrases using a possessive form.

▶ The prices this year are even lower. — This year's prices........
▶ From here it's a drive of two hours. — two hours' drive........
1 I read about it in the paper yesterday. ....
2 I just want to rest for five minutes. ....
3 It's the special offer for this month. ....
4 I'll see you in a week. ....

Reflexive pronouns

1 Introduction

Myself is a reflexive pronoun. In the sentence *I cut myself*, the words I and **myself** mean the same thing. **Myself** refers back to the subject, I.

2 Form

	FIRST PERSON	SECOND PERSON	THIRD PERSON
Singular	**myself**	**yourself**	**himself/herself/itself**
Plural	**ourselves**	**yourselves**	**themselves**

Compare **yourself** and **yourselves**.

*Emma, you can dry **yourself** with this towel.* *Vicky and Rachel, you can dry **yourselves** with these towels.*

3 The use of reflexive pronouns

Here are some examples.

*Paulo made **himself** a sandwich.* *Michelle had to force **herself** to eat.*
*We've locked **ourselves** out.* *The children watched **themselves** in the video.*

We cannot use **me**, **you**, **him**, etc. to refer to the subject. Compare these sentences.

*When the police officer came in, the gunman shot **him**.* (**him** = the police officer)
*When the police officer came in, the gunman shot **himself**.* (**himself** = the gunman)

We can use a reflexive pronoun after a preposition.

*The children are old enough to take car **of themselves**.*

But after a preposition of place, we can use **me**, **you**, **him**, etc.

*In the mirror I saw a truck **behind me**.* *Mike didn't have any money **with him**.*
*Tara thought she recognized the woman standing **next to her**.*

4 Idioms with reflexive pronouns

Look at these examples.

*We really **enjoyed ourselves**.* (= had a good time)
*I hope the children **behave themselves**.* (= behave well)
*Just **help yourself** to sandwiches.* (= take as many as you want)
*Please **make yourself at home**.* (= behave as if this was your home)
*I don't want to be left here **by myself**.* (= on my own, alone)

5 Verbs without a reflexive pronoun

Some verbs do not usually take a reflexive pronoun, although they may in other languages.

*We'd better **hurry**, or we'll be late.* NOT ~~*We'd better hurry ourselves.*~~
*Shall we **meet** at the arena?* *I **feel** uncomfortable.* *Just try to **relax**.*

Some of these verbs are: **afford**, **approach**, **complain**, **concentrate**, **decide**, **feel** + adjective, **get up**, **hurry** (**up**), **lie down**, **meet**, **remember**, **rest**, **relax**, **sit down**, **stand up**, **wake up**, **wonder**, **worry**

We do not normally use a reflexive pronoun with **change** (clothes), **dress**, and **shower**.

*Wayne **showered** and **changed** before going out.*

But we can use a reflexive pronoun when the action is difficult.

*My friend has a broken arm, but she can **dress herself**.*

Practice

A Reflexive pronouns (1–3)

Look at the pictures and write sentences with a reflexive pronoun.
Use these words: *dry*, *introduce*, *look at*, *~~photograph~~*, *teach*

▶ 
1 
2 
3 
4 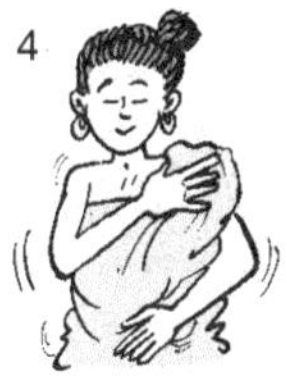

▶ He's photographing himself.
1 She ....
2 They ....
3 ....
4 ....

B Reflexive pronouns (1–3)

Complete the conversations. Write a reflexive pronoun (*myself*, *yourself*, etc.).

▶ Orin: Should I get the tickets?
Sara: It's OK. I can pay for myself.
1 Olivia: I've got lots of photos of my children.
Amanda: Yes, but you don't have many of ...., Olivia.
2 Bob: Did you have a good time at the cottage?
Pat: Well, there wasn't much going on. We had to amuse ....
3 Jared: Why did the light turn off?
Doug: It turns .... off automatically.

C Pronouns after a preposition (3)

Write the correct pronoun (e.g. *me* or *myself*).

▶ We looked up and saw a strange animal in front of us.
▶ Don't tell us the answer to the puzzle. We can figure it out by ourselves.
1 It's too bad you didn't bring your camera with ....
2 Mark talked to the woman sitting next to ....
3 The old man is no longer able to take care of ....
4 My mother likes to have all her family near ....
5 To be successful in life, you must believe in ....

D Idioms with and without reflexive pronouns (4–5)

Nancy and Steve are at Rosie and Bryan's party. Complete the conversation.
Write the verbs with or without a reflexive pronoun.

Rosie: Have you two (▶) met (met) before?
Nancy: Yes, we have. Steve and I are old friends.
Rosie: Oh, right. Well, I hope you (▶) enjoy yourselves (enjoy) tonight.
Nancy: I'm sure we will. I (1) .... (feel) like having a great time.
Rosie: Well, please (2) .... (help) to a drink. Are you OK, Steve?
Steve: Sorry, I've got this awful feeling that I have to do something very important, and I can't (3) .... (remember) what it is.
Nancy: Steve, you (4) .... (worry) too much. Come on, just (5) .... (relax).

Everyone, something, etc.

1 Introduction

Look at these examples.

__Everyone__ enjoyed the show. It was a big success.
The police searched the house but found __nothing__.
Let's find __somewhere__ to eat.
__Nobody__ came into the store all afternoon.

With **every**, **some**, and **no**, we can form words ending in **one**, **body**, **thing**, and **where**.

everyone/everybody = all the people	**everything** = all the things	**everywhere** = (in) all the places
someone/somebody = a person	**something** = a thing	**somewhere** = (in) a place
no **one/nobody** = no person	**nothing** /ˈnʌθɪŋ/ = no things	**nowhere** = (in) no places

Words ending in **thing** can also refer to actions or ideas.

__Something__ awful has happened. *You must tell me __everything__.*

2 Someone and anyone, etc.

We can also form words with **any**: **anyone**, **anybody**, **anything**, **anywhere**.

Positive:	*There's __some__one in the break room.*
Negative:	*I looked around the mall, but I didn't buy __any__thing.*
Question:	*Has __any__one seen today's newspaper?*
Offer/Request:	*Could you do __some__thing for me, please?*

We can also use words with **any** in a positive sentence.

This door is always left open. __Any__one could just walk in here.
Where shall we go? ~ __Any__where. I don't care.

In these sentences **anyone** means "it doesn't matter who," and **anywhere** means "it doesn't matter where."

3 Singular and plural

We use a singular verb after **everyone**, **something**, **anything**, etc.

__Everywhere was__ very crowded. *__No one knows__ how to start the engine.*

After words with **one** or **body**, we use the singular.

__Everyone__ is having __his__ lunch. *__Nobody__ wants to have __her__ coffee yet.*

If we don't know the person's sex, we can use two pronouns. *__Someone__ forgot __his__ or __her__ ticket.*

In spoken English, we commonly use **they/them/their** with **someone, everyone**, or **nobody** even though the verb is singular.

__Someone__ has left __their/her__ purse behind.

4 Other structures

After **everyone**, **something**, etc. we can use an adjective.

Let's go __somewhere nice__. *Is there __anything interesting__ in that magazine?*

We can also use **else**.

We always play Scrabble. Let's play __something else__. (= a different game)
Adam wore a suit, but __everyone else__ had jeans on. (= all the other people)

Words ending in **one** and **body** have a possessive form (with **'s**).

__Someone's__ cat is on our roof. *I need to be informed about __everybody's__ plans.*

Practice

A Everyone, something, etc. (1)

Complete the conversations. Write the correct words.

▶ Marta: Did you say you found ...something... in the street?
Jay: Yes, a diamond ring.

1 Claude: We all know the man is a thief, don't we?
Gerald: Yes, ... knows, but .... dares to say so publicly.

2 Mark: Were there any calls for me?
Secretary: Yes, ... called while you were out. It was strange. He refused to give his name, but he wants to discuss .... with you.

3 Fiona: Do you have any plans for the summer?
Travis: I'd like to go away .... if I can. .... I know has invited me to his cottage up north, so I may go there.

4 Danny: Has Matthew found a job yet?
Raul: No, but he's looked .... He's been to all the employment agencies. He hates the idea of sitting around doing ....

B Someone and anyone, etc. (2)

Write *someone*, *anyone*, *something*, *anything*, *somewhere*, or *anywhere*.

Chantal: Have you seen my MP3 player? I can't find it (▶) ...anywhere... .
Lisa: No, I haven't. Perhaps (1) ....'s borrowed it.
Chantal: I haven't given (2) .... permission to borrow it. It must be (3) .... in this room.
Lisa: This place is such a mess. It could be (4) ....
Chantal: I know. I can never find (5) .... when I want it.
Lisa: We'll have to do (6) .... about this mess. We'd better clean up.

C Singular and plural (3)

Choose the correct form.

▶ We had to wait because someone had lost ~~its~~/her ticket.
1 One of the police officers had injured his/their arm.
2 One of the guests had brought something wrapped in brown paper. She put it/them on the table.
3 No one likes/like going to the dentist, do he/they?
4 Everyone have/has to leave his/their bags outside.

D Other structures (4)

Rewrite the sentences using a phrase with *everyone*, *someone*, *something*, *nothing*, and *somewhere* instead of the phrases in parentheses.

▶ I'd like to buy (a nice thing). ...I'd like to buy something nice....
▶ Let's go (to another place), shall we? ...Let's go somewhere else, shall we?...
▶ I'll try to remember (the name of everyone). ...I'll try to remember everyone's name....
1 I once met (a famous person). ....
2 (A person's car) is blocking me in. ....
3 I've got (a different thing) to tell you. ....
4 We know (the opinions of all the people). ....
5 (All the other people) except you are going. ....
6 (No exciting things) ever happen here. ....

Interesting and interested

1 Introduction

JOAQUIN IS READING ABOUT UFOS.

INTERESTING

*The book is full of information. It's very **interesting**.*

The word **interesting** tells us what the book does to Joaquin—it interests him. A book can be **interesting, boring, exciting,** or **amusing,** for example.

INTERESTED

*Joaquin is very **interested** in UFOs.*

The word **interested** tells us how Joaquin feels. A person can feel **interested, bored, excited,** or **amused,** for example.

2 Adjective pairs

Here are some more examples.

-ING	-ED
*Federica told us an **amusing** story.*	*We were **amused** at Federica's story.*
*The two-hour delay was **annoying**.*	*The passengers were **annoyed** about the delay.*
*I didn't enjoy the party. It was **boring**.*	*I went to the party, but I felt **bored**.*
*This microwave has some very **confusing** instructions.*	*I got very **confused** trying to make sense of the instructions.*
*This wet weather is so **depressing**.*	*This weather makes me so **depressed**.*
*It was very **disappointing** not to get the job.*	*I was very **disappointed** not to get the job.*
*The game was really **exciting**.*	*The fans were **excited**.*
*Going for a jog with Samson is **exhausting**.*	*I'm **exhausted** after jogging all that way.*
*I thought the show about wildlife was **fascinating**.*	*I watched the show about wildlife. I was absolutely **fascinated**.*
*For one **frightening/terrifying** moment I thought I was going to fall.*	*When I got onto the roof, I felt **frightened/terrified**.*
*I just don't understand. I find the whole thing **confusing**.*	*I must say I'm **confused**. I just don't understand.*
*Lying in a hot bath is **relaxing**.*	*I feel **relaxed** when I lie in a hot bath.*
*I think the way Jessica behaved was **shocking**.*	*I was **shocked** to see Jessica behaving like that.*
*The test results were **surprising**.*	*I was **surprised** at the test results.*
*What **thrilling** news this is! Congratulations!*	*We were **thrilled** to hear your good news.*
*The trip took all day and night. They found it very **tiring**.*	*After travelling all day and night they were very **tired**.*

Practice

A Interesting and interested (1–2)

What are they saying? Write these words: ~~*depressing*~~, *exciting*, *exhausted*, *fascinating*, *interested*

▶ 

1 

2 

3 

4 

▶ This is a depressing place.

1 I'm absolutely ....

2 I'm .... in astronomy.

3 Chess is a .... game.

4 This is really ....!

B Interesting and interested (1–2)

Complete the conversation. Write the complete word in each space.

Kyle: That was an (▶) exciting (excit...) movie, wasn't it?

Max: Oh, do you think so? I'm (1) .... (surpris...) you liked it. I thought it was kind of (2) .... (disappoint...).

Kyle: Well, I didn't understand the whole story. It was (3) .... (confus...) in places. But the end was good.

Max: I was (4) .... (bor...) most of the time. I didn't find it very (5) .... (interest...).

C Interesting and interested (1–2)

Complete the conversations using a word ending in *-ing* or *-ed*.

▶ John: I'm surprised how warm it is for March.
Lannie: Yes, all this sunshine is quite surprising.

▶ Vanessa: I'm not in very good shape. I was pretty tired after climbing the mountain.
Carrie: Yes, I think everyone felt tired.

1 Josh: I think I need to relax.
Shanti: Well, lying by the pool should be ....

2 Pierre: It was annoying to lose my ticket.
Marie: You looked really .... when you had to buy another one.

3 Alejandro: The comedy show was amusing.
Jeff: Claire was certainly .... She couldn't stop laughing.

4 Ramesh: The museum was interesting, wasn't it?
Francisco: It was OK. I was very .... in those old maps.

5 Janice: I'm fascinated by these old photos.
Emmanuel: I always find it .... to see what people looked like as children.

6 Courtney: Was it a big thrill meeting Ryan Gosling?
Sara: You bet. It was just about the most .... moment of my life.

7 Pinder: You look exhausted. You should go to bed.
Kelly: Driving back from Banff was pretty ....

Adjective or adverb?

1 Introduction

Matt: *I like that song that Karen sang.*
Angie: *Yes, it's a **nice** song. And she sang it **nicely**, too.*

An adjective (**nice**) describes a noun (**song**).
*The man had a **quiet voice**.*
*Giovanna wears **expensive clothes**.*
*The runners made a **slow start**.*

An adverb (**nicely**) describes a verb (**sang**).
*The man **spoke quietly**.*
*Giovanna **dresses expensively**.*
*They **started** the race **slowly**.*
We do NOT say ~~*She sang it nice.*~~

We can use adverbs in other ways. An adverb like **really** or **very** can be combined with an adjective (**hot**) or another adverb (**carefully**).
*It was **really hot** in the sun.* *Brad checked his work **very carefully**.*
An adverb like **fortunately** or **perhaps** says something about the whole situation.
***Fortunately** nothing was stolen.* ***Perhaps** Sarah is working late.*

2 The -ly ending

We form many adverbs from an adjective + **-ly**. For example **politely**, **quickly**, **safely**.
But there are some special spelling rules.

1 We do not leave out **e**, e.g. nice → nicely
Exceptions are true → truly, whole → wholly.
2 -y → **-ily** after a consonant, e.g. easy → easily, lucky → luckily
Also **angrily**, **happily**, **heavily**, etc.
3 **-le** → -ly, e.g. possible → possibly
Also **comfortably**, **probably**, **reasonably**, **sensibly**, **terribly**, etc.
4 **-ic** → **-ically**, e.g. dramatic → dramatically
Also **automatically**, **scientifically**, etc. (Exception: **publicly**)

3 Looked nice and looked carefully

Compare these two structures.

LINKING VERB + ADJECTIVE
*Athan **was hungry**.*
*The children **seemed happy**.*
*My soup **got cold**.*
An adjective can come after a linking verb such as **be**.

ACTION VERB + ADVERB
*Athan **ate hungrily**.*
*The children **played happily**.*
*The man **stared coldly** at us.*
We use an adverb when the verb means that something happens.

Some verbs like **look**, **taste**, and **appear** can be either linking verbs or action verbs.

LINKING VERB + ADJECTIVE
*Jeff **looked angry**.*
*The medicine **tasted awful**.*
*The man **appeared** (to be) **drunk**.*

ACTION VERB + ADVERB
*He **looked carefully** at the signature.*
*Julia **tasted** the drink **nervously**.*
*A waiter **appeared suddenly**.*

Practice

A Adverbs (1–2)

This is part of a story about a spy called X. Write adverbs formed from these adjectives:
***bright*, *careful*, *fluent*, *immediate*, *patient*, *punctual*, *quiet*, *safe*, *secret*, ~~*slow*~~**

The trip took a long time because the train travelled so (▶) slowly. It was hot, and the sun shone (1) .... from a clear sky. X could only wait (2) .... for the trip to end. When the train finally arrived, he had no time to spare, so he (3) .... took a taxi to the hotel. Y was on time. She arrived (4) .... at three. No one else knew about the meeting—it was important to meet (5) .... "I had a terrible trip," said Y. "But luckily the pilot managed to land (6) ...." Her English was good, and she spoke very (7) .... X was listening (8) .... to every word. They were speaking very (9) .... in case the room was bugged.

B The -ly ending (2)

Read the information in parentheses and write the adverbs. Be careful with the spelling.

▶ (Sam's toothache was terrible.) Sam's tooth ached terribly.
1 (Julio was angry.) Julio shouted .... at the waiter.
2 (I'm happy sitting here.) I could sit here .... for hours.
3 (The machine is automatic.) The machine turns itself off ....
4 (The debate should be public.) We need to debate the matter ....
5 (Everyone was enthusiastic.) Everyone discussed the idea ....
6 (We should be reasonable.) Can't we discuss the problem ....?
7 (The building has to be secure.) Did you lock all the doors ....?

C Adverb or adjective? (1–2)

Decide what you need to say. End your sentence with an adverb ending in *-ly*.

▶ Tell the police that you can't remember the accident. It isn't very clear in your mind.
I can't remember the accident very clearly.
1 Tell your friend that the Flames won the game. It was an easy win.
....
2 Tell your boss that you've checked the figures. You've been careful.
....
3 Tell your neighbour that his dog barked at you. It was very fierce.
....
4 You are calling your friend. Tell him about the snow where you are. It's very heavy.
....

D Adverb or adjective? (1–3)

Agnes is telling Sonia about a dream she had. Choose the correct forms.

I had a (▶) strange/~~strangely~~ dream last night. I was in a garden. It was getting (1) dark/darkly, and it was (2) terrible/terribly cold. My head was aching (3) bad/badly. I was walking out of the garden when (4) sudden/suddenly I saw a man. He was sitting (5) quiet/quietly on a seat. He seemed very (6) unhappy/unhappily. He looked up and smiled (7) sad/sadly at me. I don't know why, but I felt (8) curious/curiously about him. I wanted to talk to him, but I couldn't think what to say. I just stood there (9) foolish/foolishly.

Adverbs and word order

1 Where do adverbs go?

There are three places in the sentences where an adverb can go. They are called front position (at the beginning of a sentence), mid position (close to the verb), and end position (at the end of a sentence).

FRONT		MID		END
Then	*the ship*	***slowly***	*sailed*	***away.***
Outside	*it was*	***obviously***	*raining*	***hard.***

2 Mid position

Mid position means close to the verb. Here are some examples of adverbs in mid position.

	AUXILIARY	ADVERB	AUXILIARY	MAIN VERB	
The visitors	*are*	***just***		*leaving.*	
Andrew	*has*	***always***		*liked*	*Stephanie.*
We	*don't*	***often***		*go*	*out in the evening.*
You	*should*	***never***		*take*	*unnecessary risks.*
The pictures	*have*	***definitely***	*been*	*stolen.*	
I		***really***		*hate*	*housework.*
You		***probably***		*left*	*your purse on the bus.*

The adverb comes after the first auxiliary, e.g. **are, has, don't.**
If there is no auxiliary, then the adverb comes before the main verb, e.g. **hate, left.**

Note the word order in questions.
*Has Andrew **always** liked Stephanie?* *Do you **often** go out in the evening?*

When the verb **be** is on its own, the adverb usually comes after it.
*The boss is **usually** in a bad mood.* *You're **certainly** a lot better today.*

When there is stress on the main verb **be** or on the auxiliary, then the adverb usually comes before it.
*You **certainly** <u>are</u> a lot better today.* *I **really** <u>have</u> made a mess, haven't I?*

3 Verb and object

An adverb does not usually go between the verb and the direct object.
We put it in end position, after the object.

	VERB	OBJECT	ADVERB	
Dante	*ate*	*his breakfast*	***quickly.***	NOT ~~*Dante ate quickly his breakfast.*~~
We	*played*	*volleyball*	***yesterday.***	NOT ~~*We played yesterday volleyball.*~~
I	*like*	*classical music*	***very much.***	NOT ~~*I like very much classical music.*~~

But an adverb can go before a long object.
*Detectives examined **carefully** the contents of the dead man's pockets.*

4 Adverbs of manner

An adverb of manner tells us how something happens, e.g. **noisily**, **quickly**. It usually goes in end position, but an adverb which ends in **-ly** can sometimes go in mid position.
*We asked permission **politely**.* *We **politely** asked permission.*

5 Adverbs of place and time

Adverbs and adverbial phrases of place and time usually go in end position.

*Is there a theatre **nearby**?* *People didn't have cars **then**.*
*We're meeting **by the entrance**.* *Carson wasn't very well **last week**.*
*Did you have a nice time **in Alberta**?* *I'll see you **before very long**.*

Sometimes they can go in front position.

*We're really busy this week. **Last week** we had nothing to do.*

Some short adverbs of time can also go in mid position.

*I'll **soon** find out.* *The train is **now** approaching Saskatoon.*

6 Adverbs of frequency

An adverb of frequency tells us "how often." It usually goes in mid position.

*Nada is **always** in such a hurry.* *I **sometimes** feel depressed.*
*I've **often** thought about getting married.* *Do you **usually** work late?*

Normally, **usually**, **often**, **sometimes**, and **occasionally** can also go in front or end position.

***Normally** Andy goes by subway.* *I feel depressed **sometimes**.*

Phrases like **every day**, **once a week**, or **most evenings** go in front or end position.

***Every day** we go jogging.* *Shea has driving lessons **three times a week**.*
*There's a news update **every hour**.* *We watch television **most evenings**.*

7 Sentence adverbs

A sentence adverb is a word or phrase like **certainly**, **perhaps**, **luckily**, **of course**. It says something about the situation described in the sentence. The adverb can go in front, mid, or end position.
Sometimes we put a comma after or before the adverb, especially in front or end position.

***Fortunately**, the weather stayed clear.* ***Maybe** you'll win a free vacation.*
*We'll **probably** have to line up for tickets.* *Todd was late, **of course**.*

In a negative sentence, **probably**, and **certainly** come before **won't**, **didn't**, etc.

*We **probably** won't get there in time.* *I **certainly** didn't expect a present!*

Also usually goes in mid position, but **too** and **as well** go in end position.

*Cynthia bakes delicious cakes. She **also** makes bread./She makes bread, **too/as well**.*

8 End position

There can be more than one adverb or adverbial phrase in end position. Usually a single-word adverb (e.g. **safely**) comes before a phrase (e.g. **on a small airfield**).

*They landed **safely on a small airfield**.* *I always eat **here at lunchtime**.*

When there is a close link in meaning between a verb and an adverb, then that adverb goes next to the verb. For example, with verbs of movement like **go**, **come**, and **move**, a phrase of place comes before time.

*I usually go **to bed early**.*
*Jai came **here yesterday**.*
*My parents moved **to Sherbrooke in 2005**.*

But often two adverbial phrases can go in either order.

*The concert was held **at the arts centre last night**.*
*The concert was held **last night at the arts centre**.*

Practice

A Adverbs (1–2)

Read each sentence and write down the adverb.

▶ I'm just finishing an interesting article in this magazine. just ....
1 We have to leave our dirty shoes outside. ....
2 Perhaps you have to type a password to access the site. ....
3 Someone always leaves this door open. ....
4 Obviously we aren't going to go for a walk in the rain. ....
5 The car rolled silently down the hill. ....
6 Your friend Tony works hard, doesn't he? ....

B Adverbs and their position (1–2)

Read this true story. Some adverbs are underlined. Decide if their position is front, mid, or end.

Once a man named Alvin decided to rob a bank in Montgomery, Alabama. Alvin's parents had often told him that good manners were important. So Alvin went to the bank and stood in line. He waited patiently. Soon it was his turn. He dramatically pulled out a gun and threatened the cashier. She politely told him that he was in the wrong line and should go to another counter. Alvin immediately went to the correct place and stood in line again. Suddenly the police rushed in and arrested him. Alvin was amazed. They'd caught him before he'd even committed the robbery. The moral of the story is that you shouldn't always do what your parents tell you.

	ADVERB	POSITION		ADVERB	POSITION
▶	once	front			
1	often	....	6	immediately	....
2	patiently	....	7	again	....
3	soon	....	8	suddenly	....
4	dramatically	....	9	even	....
5	politely	....	10	always	....

C Adverbs in mid position (2)

Complete the conversations using the words in parentheses. Put the adverbs in the best place.

▶ Wanda: Did you know the man who tried to steal your purse? (definitely/recognize/would)
Hannah: No, but I would definitely recognize him again.

1 Donald: That was a goal, wasn't it? (clearly/crossed)
Tomas: Yes, the puck .... the line.

2 Jean-Marc: The weather is a lot better today. (probably/rain/will)
Sharon: It said on the radio it .... later.

3 Gilbert: How do we get to Mike's place? (didn't/fully/understand)
Natalie: I don't know. I .... the directions.

4 Janice: It's quiet here today, isn't it? (usually/are)
Sabine: Yes, the neighbours .... outside on Sundays.

5 Evan: Have you been to this place before? (it/occasionally/visited)
Alain: Yes, I .... as a child.

6 Stefano: Did the computers crash this morning? (immediately/were/working)
Paul: Yes, but they .... again.

7 Maureen: Your friend's late, Saskia. (forgotten/has/obviously)
Saskia: Rachel .... that we planned to go out.

D Adverbs of frequency (2, 6)

Read what people are saying and write the information in one sentence. Put the adverb or adverbial phrase in mid or end position.

▶ Vicky: I get lost in Toronto. It always happens.
Vicky always gets lost in Toronto.

▶ Laura: The birds wake me up. It happens every morning.
The birds wake Laura up every morning.

1 Stanley: It rains when I'm on vacation. Well, usually.
....

2 Natalia: My friend visits me. She comes most weekends.
....

3 Eric: I get a pay raise. I get one every year.
....

4 Christine: I don't check my work. I never do that.
....

E Adverbs and word order (1–7)

Put the words in the correct order and write the statements. Sometimes there is more than one possible order.

▶ cleaned/every day/is/the office — The office is cleaned every day.
1 always/I've/known/your secret ....
2 afford/can't/certainly/a new car/we ....
3 didn't/far/the tourists/walk ....
4 carefully/cut/the paper/Jevani ....
5 also/can/Olivia/play/the violin ....
6 I/most days/read/the newspaper ....

F Adverbs in end position (8)

Complete these sentences from a newspaper. Put the words and phrases in the best order.

▶ The mayor has visited the show regularly since 2008 (regularly/since 2008).
1 The president died .... (at his home/peacefully).
2 The protesters marched .... (through the streets/yesterday).
3 The prime minister went .... (last year/to Mexico).
4 Marcus likes Rome. He spent a week .... (in June/there).

G Adverbs and word order (1–8)

Read the postcard from Olivia to her friend Kirsty and write the sentences. Put the adverbs in the best place.

(▶) Thank you for having us (last weekend). (1) We had a lovely time (in the country). (2) We arrived home at about eight (safely). (3) You should come and visit us (soon). (4) It's nice to see you and Tony (always). (5) You'll be able to come in the new year (maybe). (6) We'll see you (sometime).

▶ Thank you for having us last weekend.
1 ....
2 ....
3 ....
4 ....
5 ....
6 ....

Prepositions of place

1 Meanings

*The bird is **in/inside** the cage.*

*Marcie is diving **in/into** the water.*

*John is getting **out of** the car.*

*They're waiting **outside** the bank.*

*The pitcher is **on** the table.*

*The suitcase is **on top of** the cabinet.*

*Narmatha is putting her luggage **on/onto** the cart.*

*Steve is falling **off** the horse.*

*Arlynne is **at** the bus stop.*

*The table is **by/beside** the bed.*

*Jessica is sitting **next to** Andrew.*

*The airport is **near** Montreal.*

*The bus is going **to** Halifax.*

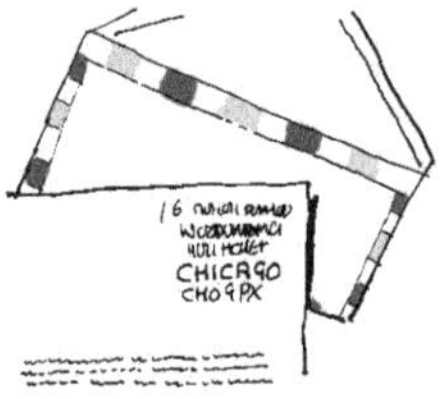

*The letter is **from** Chicago.*

*Shawn is walking **towards** the sun.*

*Kirsten is running **away from** the fire.*

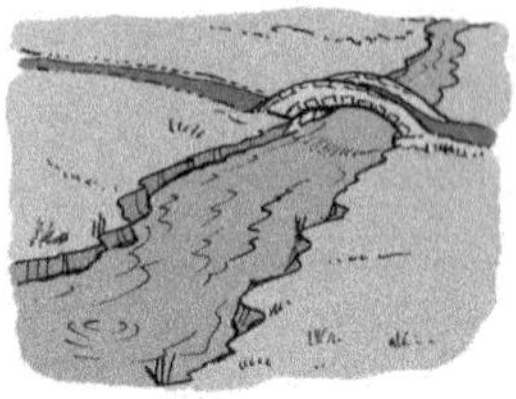

*There's a bridge **over** the river.*

*Han is **under** the car.*

*The plane is **above** the clouds.*

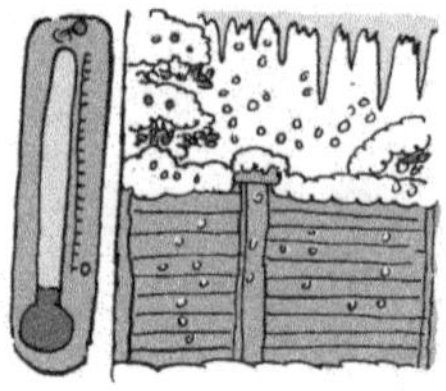

*The temperature is **below** zero.*

The cyclist is ***in front of*** *the bus.*

The cyclist is ***behind*** *the tractor.*

Rita is going ***up*** *the stairs.*

Josiah is coming ***down*** *the stairs.*

Lucy is running ***across*** *the road.*

The cars are going ***through*** *the tunnel.*

Trevor is walking ***along*** *the street.*

The car is going ***past*** *the house.*

The house is ***among*** *the trees.*

Jackson is ***between*** *Memphis and New Orleans.*

Marilyn is sitting ***opposite*** *Mohammad.*

They're running ***around/round*** *the track.*

2 Position and movement

Most of these prepositions can express either position (where something is) or movement (where it is going).

Position: *The coin* ***was under*** *the sofa.*
Movement: *The coin* ***rolled under*** *the sofa.*

Now look at these examples with **in** and **on** expressing position.

The manager was ***in*** *the office.* *The papers were* ***on*** *the floor.*

To express movement, we use **into** and **onto**, but we can also use **in** and **on**, especially in informal English.

The manager came ***in/into*** *the office.* *The papers fell* ***on/onto*** *the floor.*

At expresses position, and **to** expresses movement.

Position: *Anna* ***was at*** *the doctor's.*
Movement: *Anna* ***went to*** *the doctor's.*

Practice

A Prepositions of place (1)

Write in the prepositions. Sometimes more than one answer is correct.

▶ Sarah is getting out of the taxi.

1 Sanjit is going .... the ladder.

2 The furniture is .... the van.

3 My friend lives in an apartment .... a store.

4 The boss is coming .... the hallway.

5 There's a garage .... the house.

6 We walked .... the lake.

7 There's a statue .... the museum.

8 Bryan and Saj are walking .... the stadium.

B Prepositions of place (1)

Complete the conversations. Choose the correct preposition.

1 Amanda: I felt really afraid when I was walking home from/~~off~~ the club. The whole time I could hear someone behind/in front of me, but I didn't dare turn around.

Maddie: You must have been imagining it.

Amanda: No, I wasn't. I saw him after I'd come in across/through the gate. He was wearing a long black coat that came down well below/under his knees.

2 Carlos: You know Adam, don't you? He's very strange. He walked right along/past me yesterday as I was coming among/down the stairs, but he didn't say hello.

Frank: The other day he was sitting beside/opposite me at lunch, so I couldn't help looking at him. I said hello, but he didn't speak.

C Between, next to, and opposite (1)

Look at the plan and explain where things are. Use *between*, *next to*, or *opposite*.

► The bank is ..next to.. the gift shop.
1 The sporting goods store is .... the bank.
2 The travel agency is .... the sporting goods store and the art gallery.
3 The restaurant is .... the art gallery.
4 The gift shop is .... the bank and the restaurant.
5 The art gallery is .... the travel agency.

D Prepositions of place (1–2)

Where did the fly go? Write these prepositions: *around*, *into*, *on*, *out of*, ~~*through*~~, *under*, *up*

► The fly came in .through. the door.
1 It flew .... the chair.
2 It crawled .... the chair leg.
3 It stopped .... the desk for a moment.
4 It went .... the telephone.
5 It flew .... the drawer.
6 It went .... the window.

E Prepositions of place (1–2)

Write the correct preposition.

► Sandy was lying .on. the grass reading a book.
1 It's my vacation next week. I'm going .... Spain.
2 There was a big crowd .... the store waiting for it to open.
3 That man is an idiot. He pushed me .... the swimming pool.
4 I went .... the pharmacy just now, but I didn't notice if it was open.
5 David hurt himself. He fell .... his bike.
6 There's a café .... top of the mountain. You can have a coffee there before you go down.
7 The sheep got out .... a hole in the fence.
8 Pompeii is very .... Sorrento. It's only a short train ride.
9 There's a huge crowd. You won't find your friend .... all these people.

For, since, ago, and earlier

1 Introduction

FOR	SINCE	AGO
*Gustav has spent three hours playing a computer game. He's been sitting there **for three hours.***	*It was two o'clock when Gustav started the game. He's been playing **since two o'clock.***	*Three hours have passed since Gustav and Lydia got up from the lunch table. They finished their lunch **three hours ago.***

2 For and since with the Present Perfect

We often use **for** and **since** with the Present Perfect to talk about something continuing up to the present.

FOR	SINCE
We use **for** to say how long something has continued.	We use **since** to say when something began.
*I've been waiting **for forty minutes.***	*I've been waiting **since ten past six.***
*We've known about it **for two days.***	*We've known about it **since Monday.***
*Melanie has been living here **for a year** now.*	*Melanie has been living here **since last year.***

We can also use **for** with other tenses.

*I'**m staying** in Whitehorse **for** a year.* *We **swam for** a long time.*

We can often leave out **for** (but not from some negative sentences).

*We've had this car (**for**) six months.* *I haven't seen Casey **for** a day or two.*

3 Ago with the past

We can use the adverb **ago** to talk about a past time measured from the present.

Six months ago means six months before now.

*I passed my driving test **six months ago**.* NOT ~~*since six months*~~

*Kevin wrote to the company **weeks ago**.* *Cameron first met Mandy **a long time ago**.*

*Have you seen Emma? ~ Yes, just **a few minutes ago**.*

We put **ago** after the phrase of time. NOT ~~*ago six months*~~

4 Earlier with the Past Perfect

We use **earlier** (not **ago**) with the Past Perfect, e.g. **had done**.

*I bought a car in August. I'd passed my driving test **three months earlier**.*

(= in May, three months before August)

*Kevin finally received a reply to the email he had written **weeks earlier**.*

Practice

A For and since (1–2)

Write *for* or *since*.

Akeil: How long have you been learning English?
Jenny: Well, I studied it (▶) for five years at school, and I've been taking evening classes (1) .... last summer. That's when I finished school.
Akeil: And you're staying here (2) .... three months?
Jenny: That's right. I've been here (3) .... the end of April. I'm going to Vancouver (4) .... a week before I go home.

B For and since (1–2)

Look at the pictures and describe how long people have been there.
Use these phrases: *at his desk*, *in bed*, *in the backyard*, ~~*in the store*~~, *on the road*

▶ half an hour

1 three days

2 breakfast

3 nine o'clock

4 five hours

▶ She's been in the store for half an hour.
1 ....
2 ....
3 ....
4 ....

C For, since, or ago? (1–3)

Write a phrase with *for*, *since*, or *ago*.

▶ I got here an hour ago. ~ What? You mean you've been waiting for an hour?
1 The phone last rang at four o'clock. ~ So you've had no calls ....?
2 I haven't been to the dentist for ten years. ~ You last went to the dentist ....?
3 I last saw Rachel on Monday. ~ Haven't you seen her ....?
4 We've had six weeks without rain. ~ Yes, it hasn't rained ....
5 It's been three years since Jeanette got married. ~ Really? Has she been married ....?
6 It's been eight months since my brother had any work. ~ He lost his job ....?
7 Ivana got sick three weeks ago. ~ You mean she's been sick ...., and nobody's told me?

D Ago or earlier? (3–4)

Write *ago* or *earlier*.

▶ This movie seems familiar. Didn't we see it at the theatre about two years ago?
1 The road was wet when the accident happened. It had stopped raining only half an hour ....
2 My cellphone is working now. They fixed it a week ....
3 A young man threw himself off this bridge last year. His girlfriend had left him two days ....

Verb + object + preposition

1 Introduction

We can use some verbs in the structure: verb + object + preposition.

	VERB	OBJECT	PREPOSITION	
People	***admired***	*Cleopatra*	***for***	*her beauty.*
The trees	***protect***	*the field*	***from***	*the wind.*

In the passive, the preposition comes after the verb.

*Cleopatra was **admired for** her beauty.* *The field is **protected from** the wind.*

2 Verb + object + preposition

Here are some more examples.

*Jimmy **accused** Greg **of** cheating at cards.* *Can I **add** something **to** your list?*
*You should never **aim/point** a knife **at** someone.* *Let's **ask** someone **for** directions.*
*Janis has **invited** us **to** a party.* *I **prefer** hot weather **to** cold. I hate the cold.*
*The hotel **provided/supplied** us **with** a city map.* *Most people **regard** Emily Carr **as** a great artist.*
*Don't forget to **thank** Yuri **for** his help.* *Victor **translated** the letter **into** English.*
*The passengers **blamed/criticized** the airline **for** the delay.*
*I'll have to **borrow** the money **from** my parents.*
*If you **compare** these figures **with/to** last year's, you can see the improvement.*
*I **congratulated** Andrew **on** his excellent exam results.*
*Yvette **cut/divided/split** the pie **into** four portions.*
*The cameras **discourage/prevent** drivers **from** speeding.*
*You should **insure** your camera **against** theft. It might get stolen.*
*The two men **robbed** the woman **of** her savings. They stole $2,000 from her.*
*The restaurant was full. We **shared** a table **with** a young Quebecois couple.*
*Mike doesn't **spend** much money **on** clothes.*
*The company **suspected** one of its managers **of** selling commercial secrets.*

3 About, of, and to

We can use **about** with **tell** and **ask**.

*Did I **tell** you **about** my operation?* ***Ask** your travel agent **about** cheap flights.*

With **inform** we can use **about** or **of**.

*You should **inform** everyone **about/of** the decision.*

Look at these examples with **warn**.

*A sign **warned** drivers **about/of** the danger.* (warn **about/of** a danger)
*A sign **warned** drivers **about** the pothole.* (warn **about** something that might be dangerous)

With **remind**, there is a difference in meaning between **about** and **of**.

*Zaira **reminded** me **about** my appointment.* (= Zaira told me not to forget.)
*Zaira **reminds** me **of** my sister.* (= Zaira is like my sister.)

We can **write**, **describe**, or **explain** something **to** a person.

*I've **written** several letters **to** the company.* *The woman **described** her attacker **to** the police.*

Practice

A Verb + object + preposition (2)

This is a sports commentary at the Olympic Games.
Write the correct prepositions, e.g. ***for*****,** ***from*****.**

So Australia's Steve Brearley wins the gold medal ahead of Germany's Klaus Schliemann and Ivan Podorosky of Bulgaria. They're just congratulating Brearley (▶) ..on.. his victory. His speed over the first kilometre split the runners (1) .... two groups, and in the end it was a race between the three leaders. Brearley prevented Schliemann (2) .... overtaking him in a sprint finish. I've always regarded Brearley (3) .... a great athlete, and look how well he's done today. I would even compare him (4) .... the great Emil Kristo himself. There's no doubt now that Brearley will be invited (5) .... Oslo for the next World Championships. So the Australian runner adds another medal (6) .... his collection. And Australia is doing really well in the medals table. In fact, they share second place (7) .... the United States.

B Verb + object + preposition (2)

People are saying some surprising things.
Complete the replies using a verb + object + preposition.

▶	Dina:	I've bought a lot of books. I've spent $300.
	Jack:	What? Have you really ..spent #300 on books?..........
1	Cassandra:	I don't like wine. I prefer water.
	Jenny:	I don't believe that. Do you really ....
2	Nadine:	You heard about David's accident. Well, he's blaming Tom.
	Stephanie:	But why? Why is he ....
3	Nicola:	I gave Marie a present, but she didn't thank me.
	Alain:	Did you say she didn't ....
4	Carl:	The police say it's murder. They're accusing the history professor.
	Jamal:	What evidence do they have? How can they ....
5	Scott:	We had no towels. The hotel didn't provide them.
	Richard:	Really? Why didn't they ....
6	Catherine:	It's my sister's wedding today, but she didn't invite me.
	Ramy:	What? Do you mean she didn't ....
7	Dana:	The team won an important game, but no one congratulated them.
	Anna:	Oh? And why didn't anyone ....
8	Wendy:	A man pointed a gun. Melanie was terrified.
	Michelle:	You mean someone ....

C About, of, and to (3)

Write ***about*****,** ***of*****, or** ***to*****.**

▶ The interviewer asked Ms. Bernstein ..about.. her marathon.
1 I've told the police .... people throwing rocks at our windows.
2 That man over there reminds me .... someone I know.
3 The man explained .... the court that he had some personal problems.
4 Nikki is writing a letter .... her friends in Toronto.
5 There was a poster warning young people .... the dangers of drugs.
6 Andrea had to remind Joe .... the money he owed her.
7 We would like to inform our customers .... a number of improvements in the service we offer.

Phrasal verbs

1 Introduction

A phrasal verb is a verb + adverb, e.g. **come in, sit down, take off.** There are very many phrasal verbs in English.

Here are some adverbs which are used in phrasal verbs: **about, along, around, away, back, behind, by, down, forward, in, off, on, out, over, around, through, up**

Some of these words can also be prepositions.

2 Understanding phrasal verbs

Some phrasal verbs are easy to understand.

Frank asked Daisy to ***come in****.* *The man in front* ***turned around*** *and stared at me.*

The meanings are clear if you know the words **come, in, turn,** and **around.**

But many phrasal verbs are idiomatic. The verb + adverb has a special meaning.

Why did you ***turn down*** *such a good offer?* (= refuse)

I can't ***make out*** *whether it's a man or a woman over there.* (= see clearly)

Sometimes a phrasal verb has the same meaning as a one-word verb.

find out = discover	**leave out** = omit	**send out** = distribute
go back = return	**make up** = invent (a story)	**throw away** = discard
go on = continue	**put off** = postpone	**turn up** = arrive

The phrasal verb is usually more informal than the one-word verb.

3 Word order with phrasal verbs

When a phrasal verb has an object, the object can go either before or after the adverb.

	VERB	OBJECT	ADVERB			VERB	ADVERB	OBJECT
Daisy	***took***	*her coat*	***off.***	OR	*Daisy*	***took***	***off***	*her coat.*
I	***wrote***	*the number*	***down.***	OR	*I*	***wrote***	***down***	*the number.*
Who	***let***	*the cat*	***out?***	OR	*Who*	***let***	***out***	*the cat?*

A long object goes after the adverb.

The thieves have ***carried out a number of bank robberies*** *in the last few months.*

Why don't you ***try on that dress in the window?***

A pronoun (e.g. **it, them**) always goes before the adverb.

Daisy felt hot in her coat, so she ***took it off.***

NOT ~~*She took off it.*~~

There have been a number of robberies. The police know who ***carried them out.***

NOT ~~*The police know who carried out them.*~~

Practice

A Understanding phrasal verbs (1–2)

Work out the meaning of these phrasal verbs and put them in the correct sentences: *come back*, *~~come in~~*, *cut out*, *fall over*, *get on*, *give away*, *go away*, *~~let in~~*, *lie down*, *pay back*, *stay in*, *take back*. (Use a dictionary if you need to.)

▶ Hello. Nice to see you. Come in and sit down.
▶ I didn't have a key, but luckily someone was there to let me in.
1 Can't we go out somewhere? I don't want to .... all evening.
2 Could you lend me ten dollars? I'll .... you .... on Friday.
3 That ladder doesn't look safe. Make sure it doesn't ....
4 I was feeling so tired I had to .... on the bed for a while.
5 There was an article in the newspaper that I wanted to .... and keep.
6 Mark's out, and I don't know when he's going to ....
7 The driver unlocked the bus so that the passengers were able to ....
8 I'll have to .... these books .... to the library.
9 Your brother was being annoying, so I told him to ....
10 In order to get publicity, the company decided to .... some of the new chocolate bars for free.

B Phrasal verbs (2)

Write a phrasal verb that means the same as the verb in parentheses. Use the correct form of the phrasal verb.

Rose: I (▶) found out (discovered) what the problem is with the test.
Dalia: Oh, good. Tell me.
Rose: When they printed the papers, they (1) .... (omitted) a page. No one noticed until the papers had all been (2) .... (distributed). Now they'll have to (3) .... (discard) all the papers and (4) .... (postpone) the exam.
Dalia: Are you sure you haven't (5) .... (invented) this whole story?
Rose: It's true—I promise. And isn't it good news?
Dalia: I don't know about that. It means we'll have to (6) .... (continue) studying.

C Word order with phrasal verbs (3)

Complete the sentences by writing the phrasal verbs. You will have to leave some of the spaces empty. Sometimes more than one answer is correct.

▶ The sweater was full of holes, so I threw it away (threw away).
▶ I put up (put up) that picture we bought last week.
1 There's always litter here. No one ever .... it .... (pick up).
2 It's cold now. I think I'll .... my coat .... (put on).
3 Which apartment is Gina's? We should .... that .... (find out).
4 Daniel has to go to the college to .... his project .... (hand in).
5 I can't remember the address. I wish I'd .... it .... (write down).
6 Doug is trying to .... all the money he's just lost .... (win back).
7 I'm not going to have time to .... these dishes .... (put away).
8 If you don't know the number, you can .... it .... (look up) online.
9 There was an accident that .... all the traffic coming into town .... (held up).
10 The words "expect" and "except" are so similar that I keep .... them .... (mix up).

Reported speech: person, place, and time

1 Introduction

It's Friday afternoon. Will is at Paolo's apartment. Tom has decided to have a party for all his friends.

A few minutes later Adeel has arrived at the apartment. Now Will is reporting what Paolo said. So instead of Paolo's words, **I'm having**, Will says **he's having.**

The next day Will is talking to Lynda. Now Will is in a different place from where Paolo first told him about the party. So instead of **here**, he says **at his apartment.** And a day has passed since he first heard about it. It is now the day of the party. So instead of **tomorrow night**, Will says **tonight**.

2 Changes in reported speech

Changes from direct speech to reported speech depend on changes in the situation. We may have to make changes when we are reporting something another person has said, or when we report it in a different place or at a different time. Here are some typical changes.

Person:	I	→	he/she
	my	→	his/her
Place:	here	→	there, at the apartment
Time:	now	→	then, at the time
	today	→	that day, on Monday, etc.
	yesterday	→	the day before, the previous day
	tomorrow	→	the next/following day, on Saturday, etc.
	this week	→	that week
	last week	→	the week before, the previous week
	an hour ago	→	an hour before/earlier

Practice

A Changes in reported speech (1–2)

Read what each person says and then complete the sentences.

▶	Rashad:	Dean told me on Friday that he'd had a job interview the previous day. Dean had a job interview on ...Thursday.................... .
1	John:	Raissa tells me I need a haircut. .... needs a haircut.
2	Rena:	My brother told me in 2009 that he expected to become a manager the following year. Rena's brother expected that he would become a manager in ....
3	Ali:	I wanted to see Mark in April, but he said he was very busy that month. Mark was very busy in ....
4	Hiroshi:	I saw Justin last week. He said he'd given up smoking the week before. Justin gave up smoking .... ago.

B Changes of person (1–2)

Write the missing words.

▶

C Changes of place and time (1–2)

Write *here*, *that day*, *the day before*, ~~*the next day*~~, *the week before*.

▶	Shauna (a week ago): You (today):	I'm taking my driving test tomorrow. When I saw Shauna, she said she was taking her driving test the next day.
1	Elisa (two days ago): You (today):	I've only had this new computer since yesterday. Elisa said she'd only had the new computer since ....
2	Francisco (a week ago): You (today):	I'm meeting a friend at the airport later today. Francisco said he was meeting a friend at the airport later ....
3	Mark (in the street): You (in the office):	I'll see you at the office. Mark said he would see me ....
4	Lina (a month ago): You (today):	The conference was last week. Lina told me the conference had taken place ....

Reported speech: the tense change

1 When do we change the tense?

After a past-tense verb (e.g. **said**), there is often a tense change.

*"It really **is** cold today."* → *Lydia said it **was** cold.*

If the statement is still up to date when we report it, then we have a choice.
We can either leave the tense the same, or we can change it.

*You said you **like/liked** chocolate.* *Claire told me her father **owns/owned** a racehorse.*
*Farrah said she**'s** going/she **was** going to Winnipeg in April.*

We can say that Farrah *is* going to Winnipeg because it *is* still true that she will go there.

If the statement is no longer up to date, then we change the tense.

*Claire once told me that her father **owned** a racehorse.* (He may no longer own one.)
*Farrah said she **was** going to Winnipeg in April.* (Now it is May.)

Now Farrah's trip is over, so it is no longer true that she *is* going to Winnipeg.

We usually change the tense if we think the statement is untrue or may be untrue.

*You said you **liked** chocolate, but you aren't eating any.*
*The prime minister claimed that Parliament **had** made the right decision.*

2 Is → was, like → liked, etc.

Look at these examples of the tense change.

DIRECT SPEECH		REPORTED SPEECH
*"Brodie **is** working."*	→	*Kelly said Brodie **was** working.*
*"The windows **aren't** locked."*	→	*Marc told me the windows **weren't** locked.*
*"I**'ve** fixed the shelves."*	→	*Sean said he**'d** fixed the shelves.*
*"It**'s** been raining."*	→	*We noticed it **had** been raining.*
*"We**'ve** got plenty of time."*	→	*Raina insisted they **had** plenty of time.*
*"We **like** the apartment."*	→	*The couple said they **liked** the apartment.*

If the verb phrase is more than one word (e.g. **is working**), then the first word changes, e.g. ***is** working* → ***was** working, **have** fixed* → ***had** fixed, **don't** know* → ***didn't** know.*
If the verb is already in the past tense, then it can stay the same or change to the Past Perfect.

*"We **came** by car."*	→	*They said they **came**/they **had come** by car.*
*"Sorry. I **wasn't** listening."*	→	*I admitted I **wasn't** listening/**hadn't been** listening.*

If the verb is Past Perfect, it stays the same.

*"My money **had run** out."*	→	*Stefano said his money **had run** out.*

3 Modal verbs: can → could, etc.

Can, **may**, and **will** change to **could**, **might** and **would**.

*"You **can** sit over there."*	→	*The flight attendant said we **could** sit here.*
*"I **may** go to St. John's again."*	→	*Claire said she **might** go to St. John's again.*
*"I**'ll** help if you like."*	→	*Erdem said he **would** help.*

Could, **might**, **ought to**, **should**, and **would** stay the same. But **must** can change to **have to**.

*"Geeta **would** love a vacation."*	→	*Alain thought Geeta **would** love a vacation.*
*"I **must** finish this report."*	→	*Toni said she **must** finish/**had to** finish the report.*

Practice

A When do we change the tense? (1)

Write *is* or *was*. Sometimes both are possible.

▶ I heard today that the house ...is... for sale. I wonder who will buy it.
▶ I saw Matt yesterday. He said he .was. on his way to visit his sister.
1 This wallet is made of plastic, not leather. Why did you tell me it .... leather?
2 We had to hurry yesterday morning. Just as we arrived at the train station, we heard an announcement that our train .... about to leave.
3 I saw Vera just now. She said her tooth .... still aching.
4 I'm surprised Kevin lost. I thought he .... much better at tennis than Dave.
5 When he spoke to reporters yesterday, Mr. Rampaul said that the company .... now in a much better financial position.

B The tense change (2)

Complete the replies. The second speaker is surprised at what he or she hears.

▶ Chester: Emma and I are getting married.
Josie: Really? But you said last week .you weren't getting married.............
▶ Sangita: I like pop music more than classical music.
Clara: I'm sure you told me .you liked classical music best.............
1 Stanley: I haven't finished my project.
Maddie: Haven't you? I thought you said ....
2 April: I'm on a diet.
Kathy: But you told me ....
3 Eric: I enjoy parties.
Bryan: But I remember you saying ....
4 Dean: I'm applying for the job.
Liem: I thought you told me ....

C The tense change (2–3)

A play called *Don't Look Now!* has just closed after five years in Toronto's theatre district. Here's what the critics said when it opened five years ago.

▶ "It's a fantastic show." *The Daily Mail*
▶ "You'll love it." *Toronto Today*
1 "The production is amazing." *The Times*
2 "I can't remember a funnier show." *Steve Devine*
3 "It made me laugh." *Sharida Birani*
4 "You must see it." *The Canadian Globe*
5 "It will be a great success." *The City Star*
6 "You might die laughing." *The Express*
7 "It's the funniest show I've ever seen." *Marcel Chauvin*
8 "You shouldn't miss it." *Entertainment Monthly*

Now report what the critics said.

▶ The Daily Mail said it was a fantastic show.
▶ Toronto Today said people would love it.
1 ....
2 ....
3 ....
4 ....
5 ....
6 ....
7 ....
8 ....

Reported questions

1 Wh- questions

We can report questions with verbs like **ask, wonder**, or **want to know**. Look first at these **wh-** questions.

DIRECT QUESTION		REPORTED QUESTION
*"**When** did you start acting, Ava?"*	→	*Guy **asked** Ava **when** she started acting.*
*"**What**'s the time?"*	→	*I just **asked what** the time is.*
*"**Which** way is the post office?"*	→	*Someone **wants to know which** way the post office is.*
*"**How** can we find out?"*	→	*I was **wondering how** we can find out.*
*"**Where** can we eat?"*	→	*They're **asking where** they can eat.*

Wh- questions have a word like **when, what, which**, or **how** both in direct speech and in reported speech.

2 Yes/no questions

DIRECT QUESTION		REPORTED QUESTION
*"Has the taxi arrived yet?" ~ "**No**, not yet."*	→	*Someone was **wondering if/whether** the taxi has arrived yet.*
*"Can we take photos?" ~ "**Yes**, of course."*	→	*The visitors **want to know if/whether** they can take photos.*
*"Is there a café nearby?" ~ "**No**."*	→	*Daniel **asked if/whether** there was a café nearby.*

Reported yes/no questions have **if** or **whether**.

3 Word order

In a reported question, the subject comes before the verb, as in a statement.

*Guy asked Ava when **she started** acting.*

NOT ~~*Guy asked Ava when did she start acting.*~~

*Someone was wondering if **the taxi has** arrived yet.*

NOT ~~*Someone was wondering if has the taxi arrived yet.*~~

4 Asking for information

To ask politely for information, we sometimes use a reported question after a phrase like **Could you tell me ...?** or **Do you know ...?**

***Could you tell me** what time the concert starts?*

***Do you know** if there's an elevator in the building?*

***Have you any idea** how much a taxi would cost?*

Note the word order **a taxi would cost** (see part 3).

5 The tense change: is → was, etc.

In reported speech there are often changes to the tense, to pronouns, and so on.
This depends on changes to the situation since the words were spoken.
For details see pages 88 and 90. Here are some examples of the tense change.

*"What**'s** the problem?"*	→	*We asked what the problem **was**.*
*"How much money do you **have**, Ivan?"*	→	*I was wondering how much money Ivan **had**.*
*"**Does** Nigel **need** a lift?"*	→	*Pierre asked if Nigel **needed** a lift.*
*"**Can** you ski?"*	→	*They asked me if I **could** ski.*

Practice

A Reported questions (1–3)

These people are at the tourist information centre. What do they want to know?

▶ She wants to know what the most interesting sights are.
▶ He wants to know if the centre has a city map.
1 ....
2 ....
3 ....
4 ....

B Asking for information (4)

You need information. Ask for it using *Could you tell me ...?* or *Do you know ...?*

▶	Where is the washrooms? (tell)	Could you tell me where the washroom is?
1	Can I park here? (know)	....
2	How long does the movie last? (tell)	....
3	How often do the buses run? (know)	....
4	Are we allowed to smoke? (know)	....
5	What time is the flight? (tell)	....
6	How much does a ticket cost? (tell)	....

C The tense change (5)

Edwin Poon is talking to a reporter about his business career. He can still remember his first job interview after graduating.

	Interviewer:	Barry:
▶	"Where do you live?"	The interviewer asked me where I lived.
▶	"Have you worked before?"	She asked me if I had worked before.
1	"Why do you want the job?"	She wanted to know ....
2	"How did you hear about it?"	I remember she asked ....
3	"Are you hard-working?"	She wondered ....
4	"Can you work on Saturdays?"	Then she asked me ....
5	"How will you travel to work?"	She wanted to know ....
6	"Do you have a bicycle?"	And she asked me ....
7	"How much do you hope to earn?"	She also asked ....
8	"When can you start?"	And finally she asked ....

Reported requests, offers, etc.

1 Reported orders and requests

We can use the structure **tell/ask someone to do something.**

DIRECT SPEECH		REPORTED SPEECH
"Please move this car."	→	*A police officer* ***told me to move*** *the car.*
"You really must be careful."	→	*Nancy is always* ***telling Steve to be*** *careful.*
"Would you mind turning the music down?"	→	*We* ***asked our neighbours to turn*** *the music down.*

The negative is **tell/ask someone not to do something.**

"You must not leave the door unlocked."	→	*Mr. Neice* ***told Josiah not to leave*** *the door unlocked.*
"Please don't wear those boots in the house."	→	***I asked you not to wear*** *those boots in the house.*

We can also use the structure **ask to do something.**

"Can I see your ticket, please?"	→	*The inspector* ***asked to see*** *my ticket.*

We use **ask for** when someone asks to have something.

"Can I have some brochures, please?"	→	***I asked*** *(the guide) for some brochures.*

It is also possible to report an order or request like this.

A police officer told me (that) I had to move the car.
We asked our neighbours if they would mind turning the music down.

2 Reported offers, suggestions, etc.

We can use **agree**, **offer**, **promise**, **refuse**, and **threaten** with a **to**-infinitive.

DIRECT SPEECH		REPORTED SPEECH
"We'll pay for the damage."	→	*We* ***offered to pay*** *for the damage.*
"I'll definitely finish it by the end of next week."	→	*You* ***promised to finish*** *the work by the end of this week.*

We can also use an object + **to**-infinitive after **advise**, **invite**, **remind**, and **warn.**

"I think you should take a taxi."	→	*Mark* ***advised us to take*** *a taxi.*
"Don't forget to call me."	→	***I reminded Candace to call*** *me.*

We can use an **-ing** form after **admit**, **apologize for**, **insist on**, and **suggest.**

"I really need a break."	→	*Paul* ***insisted on taking*** *a break.*
"Should we have a picnic?"	→	*Claire* ***suggested having*** *a picnic.*

3 **Admit that, insist that**, etc.

We can use a clause with **that** after **admit**, **advise**, **agree**, **insist**, **promise**, **remind**, **suggest**, and **warn.**

Jean-Paul ***admitted (that)*** *he had forgotten to get groceries.*
Kim ***insisted (that)*** *we all go to her house for coffee.*
You ***promised (that)*** *you would finish the work by the end of this week.*
I ***warned*** *you* ***(that)*** *Tyra's dog is very aggressive.*

Practice

A Reported orders and requests (1)

Manny isn't feeling very happy. Everyone has been telling him what to do. Report the orders and requests.

▶ His mother: Can you weed my garden, please, Manny?
His mother asked him to weed her garden.

1 The doctor: You must get more exercise.
....

2 His boss: Would you mind not playing computer games at the office?
....

3 A police officer: You can't park your car on Queen Street.
....

4 Shanti: Could you hang these pictures, please, Manny?
....

B Reported offers, suggestions, etc. (2)

Complete the sentences. Report what was said.

▶ Would you like to stay for lunch, Milena?

▶ All right. I won't talk about hockey.

1 You ought to take a break, Craig.

2 I'm sorry I forgot to get groceries.

3 Why don't we sing a few songs?

4 Don't forget to mail that letter, Fone-Ning.

5 Yes, I made a mistake.

6 Sam! Don't touch those wires!

▶ Sarah invited *Milena to stay for lunch.*
▶ Phil agreed *not to talk about hockey.*
1 Mathieu advised ....
2 Mike apologized ....
3 Katie suggested ....
4 Jeremy reminded ....
5 Mr. Tan admitted ....
6 Jerusha warned ....

C Admit that, insist that, etc. (3)

Combine each pair of sentences using *that*.

▶ The roads were dangerous. The police warned us.
The police warned us that the roads were dangerous.

1 Everything will be ready on time. The builders have promised.
....

2 We have to check the figures carefully. The boss insists.
....

3 Warren's story wasn't completely true. He's admitted it.
....

4 Bella's train was about to leave. Gino reminded her.
....

Relative clauses with **who, which,** and **that**

1 Introduction

Shannon: *I saw Megan the other day.*
Alison: *Megan? The girl* ***who plays the piano****?*
Shannon: *No, that's Milania. Megan is the student* ***who dropped out of college****, the one* ***who never did any studying****. She's working at Davidson's now, the store* ***that sells very expensive clothes****.*

The relative clauses in this conversation identify which person or thing we are talking about. The clause **who plays the piano** tells us which girl Alison means. The clause **that sells very expensive clothes** tells us which store Shannon means.

Sometimes we can use an adjective or a phrase to identify someone or something.
Adjective: *the* ***tall*** *girl* *the* ***new*** *student* *the* ***red*** *car*
Phrase: *the man* ***in the suit*** *the store* ***on the corner*** *the woman* ***with red hair***
But when we need a longer explanation, we can use a relative clause.
Relative clause: *the woman* ***who gets up early*** *the car* ***that broke down***

2 **Who, which,** and **that**

The relative pronouns **who**, **which**, and **that** go after the noun and at the beginning of the relative clause.
Who refers to people.

Joel is the ***man who*** *owns that enormous dog.* *I don't like* ***people who*** *tell jokes all the time.*
The little ***girl who*** *sat next to me on the bus ate candy the whole way.*
Sarah is pretty annoyed with the ***person who*** *stole her cellphone.*

In spoken English, we sometimes use **that** instead of **who**.

Jake is the ***man that*** *plays the guitar.*
The ***woman that*** *lived here before us is a famous author.*

That and **which** refer to things. **That** is more common than **which**, especially in conversation.

The ***car that*** *won the race looked very futuristic, didn't it?*
They've recaptured all the ***animals that*** *escaped from the zoo.*
The children saw the actual ***spacecraft that*** *landed on the moon.*

Which can be a little formal.

There are several ***restaurants which*** *serve Sunday brunch.*
Is Polar Inc. the ***company which*** *was taken over last year?*

We do not use another pronoun like **he** or **it** with the relative pronoun.

NOT ~~*the man who he owns that enormous dog*~~
NOT ~~*the actual spacecraft that it landed on the moon*~~

In all these sentences **who**, **which**, and **that** are the subject of the relative clause.

Practice

A Identifying (1)

Look at the information and identify which one is meant.
Use the shortest way of identifying where possible, e.g. *the tall boy*, not *the boy who is tall*.

▶ the boy (he is tall) → the tall boy
▶ the man (he has a beard) → the man with a beard
▶ the woman (she plays golf) → the woman who plays golf
1 the young man (he is at the door) → ....
2 the man (he plays his stereo at night) → ....
3 the woman (she is very thin) → ....
4 the girl (she has green eyes) → ....
5 the young woman (she is in the office) → ....
6 the man (he drives a taxi) → ....
7 the young man (he is smart) → ....
8 the student (she failed all her exams) → ....

B Who, which, and that (2)

Complete the conversation. Write *who*, *which*, or *that*.
There is always more than one possible answer.

Ricardo: Shall we have something to eat?
Preema: Yes, but not here. I don't like restaurants (▶) that get too crowded. I'm not one of those people (▶) who can eat in a loud, stuffy room.
Ricardo: There's another restaurant over there.
Preema: It looks expensive—one of those places (1) .... charge very high prices. The only customers (2) .... can afford to eat there are business executives (3) .... get their expenses paid. Anyway, I can't see a menu. I'm not going into a restaurant (4) .... doesn't display a menu.
Ricardo: We just passed a café (5) .... sells lunch.
Preema: Oh, I didn't like the look of that.
Ricardo: You're one of those people (6) .... are never satisfied, aren't you?

C Relative clauses (1–2)

Combine the information to create news items. Make the sentence in parentheses into a relative clause with *who* or *which*. Start each sentence with *the*, e.g. *The man ...*

▶ A man has gone to prison. (He shot two police officers.)
The man who shot two police officers has gone to prison.

1 An earthquake caused a lot of damage. (It occurred in Chile.)
....

2 A scientist has won the Nobel Prize. (He discovered a new planet.)
....

3 A hockey player has been suspended for ten games. (He injured his opponent.)
....

4 A little girl has been found safe and well. (She had been missing since Tuesday.)
....

5 A company has laid off thousands of employees. (It owns Car-Co Manufacturing.)
....

6 A 75-year-old woman now wants to swim across Lake Ontario. (She went bungee jumping.)
....

Relative structures with **whose**, **what**, and **it**

1 Whose

Nikki: *What I'd really like is a job in television.*
Andy: *The other day I met a man **whose sister** works in television.*
Nikki: *Who? What's her name?*
Andy: *Oh, I don't know. She's the woman **whose car** Tomas crashed into.*

Here **whose sister** means *his* sister (the sister of the man Andy met), and **whose car** means *her* car (the car belonging to the woman). Here are some more examples.

*Someone **whose bicycle** had been stolen was reporting it to the police.*
*Sidney Crosby is the man **whose goal** won the game for Canada.*

We use **whose** mainly with people, e.g. **someone, the man.** But sometimes it goes with other nouns.

*Which is the Asian **country whose** economy is growing the fastest?*
*Around the corner was a **building whose** windows were all broken.*
*Sasha was looking after a **dog whose** leg had been broken in an accident.*

2 What

We use the relative pronoun **what** without a noun in front of it.

*The store didn't have **what** I wanted.* (= the thing that I wanted)
***What** we saw gave us quite a shock.* (= the thing that we saw)

We can also use **what** to give emphasis to a word or phrase, to make it more important. Compare these examples.

NEUTRAL	EMPHATIC
Rachel's stereo kept me awake.	***What** kept me awake was **Rachel's stereo**.*
Nikki is looking for a job in television.	***What** Nikki is looking for is **a job in television**.*
I want to make a fresh start.	***What** I want to do is **make a fresh start**.*
They booked a vacation together.	***What** they did was **book a vacation together**.*

3 It

We also use **it** + **be** + a relative clause to give emphasis.

NEUTRAL	EMPHATIC
Yan had an accident.	***It was Yan** who had an accident (not David).*
The computer gives me a headache.	***It's the computer** that gives me a headache.*
I'm eating chocolate cake.	***It's chocolate cake** (that) I'm eating.*
Mike's uncle died on Thursday.	***It was on Thursday** that Mike's uncle died.*

We must include a pronoun when it refers to the subject of the relative clause (e.g. ***who** had an accident*). If it refers to the object (e.g. ***that** I'm eating*), then we can leave it out.

Practice

A Who or whose? (1)

You are reading a crime story. One of these characters has murdered the industrialist Maurice Le Mans. Read the detective's notes and write a sentence about each character. Use a relative clause with *who* or *whose*.

▶ George Paxton, company director: he had an argument with Maurice
George is the company director who had an argument with Maurice.

▶ Vera Stojko, politician: her sister once worked for Maurice
Vera is the politician whose sister once worked for Maurice.

1 Felix Reeves, journalist: his tape recorder was stolen
....

2 Graham Wilshaw, architect: he knew Maurice in school
....

3 Frank Lafferty, farmer: Maurice bought his land
....

4 Sal Politano, lawyer: he looked after Maurice's interests
....

5 Sonia Goldman, house guest: her fingerprints were on the doorknob
....

B What (2)

Mr. Azad is telling a group of managers how to run a business successfully. He emphasizes the underlined words using *what*.

▶ You must pay attention to the details.
What you must pay attention to are the details.

1 You have to think about your profit.
....

2 You must know the needs of your customers.
....

3 You should work towards a realistic target.
....

4 You need to plan ahead.
....

C It (3)

Students competing in a trivia challenge are answering some questions.
Read each question and answer and write a sentence with *it* + *be* + a relative clause.

▶ Who invented the radio? ~ Marconi.
It was Marconi who invented the radio.

1 When did Cartier first sail to Canada? ~ In 1534.
It was in 1534 that ....

2 What sport does Chelsea Stewart play? ~ Soccer.
It's ....

3 Where did the Olympic Games first take place? ~ In Greece.
....

4 Which is closest to the sun: Venus or Mercury? ~ Mercury.
....

Conditionals

1 First, Second, and Third Conditionals

BEFORE THE GAME.

AFTER THE GAME.

There are three main types of conditional. Study the examples.
First (Real Conditional): **if** … the Simple Present … **will/can/might**, etc.
If we win today, we'll make it to the playoffs. (We may win, or we may not.)
Second (Unreal Conditional): **if** … Simple Past … **would/could/might**
If Tremblay was on the team, I'd feel more confident. (Tremblay isn't on the team.)
Third (Past Conditional): **if** … Past Perfect … **would have/could have/might have**
***If** Tremblay **had** played, we'**d have** won.* (Tremblay didn't play.)

Here are some more examples with different verb forms.

First	*If **I'm** going shopping, **I'll** need some money.*
	*If the party downstairs **has** finished, we **might** be able to get some sleep.*
	*You **should** stay in bed if you **feel** sick.*
Second	*If I **didn't** like this pie, I **wouldn't** eat it.*
	*If the DVD player **was** working, we **could** watch a movie.*
	*The alarm **might** go off if we **tried** to get in through a window.*
Third	*If we'**d dropped** the piano, it **would have** been a disaster.*
	*If Sonia **had gone** to the amusement park with us last week, she **might have** enjoyed it.*
	*We **could have** given you a lift if we'**d known** you were coming this way.*

2 Other conditional sentences

As well as the three main types, there are other types of conditional sentences.
For example, we can use two present-tense verbs.
*If you **call** this number, no one **answers**.*

We can also use a present-tense verb and an imperative.
*If you **need** any help, just **ask**.* *If you **drink, don't drive**.*

We can use **be going to.**
*If it'**s going to** rain, I'd better take an umbrella.*
*If they try to cut down the trees, there'**s going to** be a big protest.*

We can mix the Second and Third Conditionals.
*If Luca **had booked** a table, we **wouldn't** be standing here in a lineup.*
*If you **needed** help, you **should have** asked me.*

Practice

A First, Second, and Third Conditionals (1)

Match the sentences and join them with *if*. Decide what types of conditional they are.

▶	I went to bed earlier.	I'll try to follow them.
1	The twins had worn different clothes.	You might not be warm enough.
2	You tell me what the instructions say.	I wouldn't have bought it.
3	People used public transportation.	~~I wouldn't sleep.~~
4	You don't wear a sweater.	There'd be less pollution.
5	I hadn't seen the product advertised.	We could have told them apart.

▶ If I went to bed earlier, I wouldn't sleep. .... Second

1 ....

2 ....

3 ....

4 ....

5 ....

B First, Second, and Third Conditionals (1)

Adam is a music student. He rents an apartment from Mr. Onassis. Write the correct forms.

Mr. Onassis: Can't you stop playing that trumpet? You're making an awful noise.

Adam: Well, if (▶) I don't practise (I/not practise), I won't pass my music exam.

Mr. Onassis: But why at night? It's after midnight. If (1) .... (you/play) it in the daytime, (2) .... (I/not/hear) you because I'd be at work. If (3) .... (you/tell) me about this trumpet when you first came here, (4) .... (I/not/rent) you the apartment. I'm afraid it's becoming a problem. If (5) .... (you/not/play) so loudly, (6) .... (it/not/be) so bad.

Adam: I'm sorry, but you can't play a trumpet quietly.

Mr. Onassis: If (7) .... (I/realize) a year ago what you were going to do, then (8) .... (I/throw) you out long ago. If (9) .... (you/go on) making this noise at night, (10) .... (I/have) to ask you to leave.

C Conditionals (1–2)

What might you say in these situations? Use a conditional sentence.

▶ You think Julie should reserve a seat on the train. The alternative is having to take the bus.
If Julie doesn't reserve a seat on the train, she'll have to take the bus.

1 You didn't know how unpopular Jason was when you invited him to your party.
....

2 Warn your friend not to put too many cans into the plastic bag or it'll break.
....

3 You don't have a pen, so you can't write down the address.
....

4 You should have started your project earlier. You're so far behind now.
....

5 Your friend might need some help. If so, tell her to call you.
....

6 The automatic result of the door opening is the fan coming on.
....

But, although, in spite of, whereas, etc.

1 But, although, and however

We can join two sentences with **but**.

*The café was crowded, **but** we found a table.* *Sanjit has a car, **but** he doesn't drive it often.*

But expresses a contrast or conflict between two ideas. We can also use **although**.

***Although** the café was crowded, we found a table.* ***Although** Sanjit has a car, he doesn't drive it often.*

The clause with **although** can come at the end.

*We found a table, **although** the café was crowded.*

However is a little formal.

*The new system was supposed to be more efficient. **However**, in practice it caused chaos./In practice, **however**, it caused chaos.*

2 Though and even though

Though is informal. It means the same as **although**.

***Though/Although** I liked the sweater, I decided not to buy it.*

We can also use **though** at the end of a sentence.

*I liked the sweater. I decided not to buy it, **though**.*

Even though is stronger, more emphatic than **although**.

*Alvaro looked great, **even though** he'd been playing rugby.*

***Even though** you dislike Jessica, you should try to be nice to her.*

3 In spite of and despite

We use **in spite of** before a noun or before the **-ing** form of a verb.

*Monique wanted to report on the war **in spite of** the danger.*

*Riyaad went on working **in spite of** feeling sick.*

We use **despite** in exactly the same way as **in spite of** and with the same meaning.

*She wanted to go **despite** the danger.* *He went on working **despite** feeling sick.*

4 In spite of and although

IN SPITE OF	ALTHOUGH
*I'm no better **in spite of** the pills/**in spite of** taking the pills.*	*I'm no better, **although** I've taken the pills.*
*Angel wants to fly **in spite of** her fear/**in spite of** feeling afraid.* NOT ~~in spite of she feels afraid~~	*Angel wants to fly, **although** she feels afraid.*

We can use **in spite of the fact (that)** in the same way as **although**.

*I'm no better **in spite of the fact that** I've taken the pills.*

5 Whereas, while, and on the other hand

We use these words to express a comparison between two ideas.

*Jeff is a talented curler, **whereas** Diane is not.*

*Yesterday it was freezing cold, **while** today it's quite warm.*

*The house is conveniently located. **On the other hand**, there's a lot of noise from the traffic./There is, **on the other hand**, a lot of noise from the traffic.*

Sometimes either **but** or **whereas** is possible.

*The red pills make me feel sick, **but/whereas** the blue ones don't.*

Practice

A But (1)

Complete each sentence with *but* and one of these clauses:

~~it didn't break~~*, *it's actually very modern*, *no one laughed*, *she turned it down

▶ I dropped the dish, but it didn't break.

1 The house looks old, ...

2 Emma was offered a job, ...

3 The joke was funny, ...

B In spite of and although (4)

Write *although* or *in spite of*.

▶ My sister got the job, although she didn't expect to.

1 .... I told the absolute truth, no one would believe me.

2 Jesse forgot his passport .... having it on his list.

3 .... it was sunny, it was a cold day.

4 The goods were never delivered .... the promise we had received.

5 Hong asked Ruth to marry him .... the fact that he's a lot older than she is.

C But, although, however, even though, in spite of, and despite (1–4)

Complete the report by writing the correct linking words. There is always more than one possible answer.

(▶) Although the ground was very wet, it was decided to go ahead with the baseball game. The visiting team won (1) .... not playing very well. (2) .... the poor conditions, the home team made some great plays, (3) .... they just couldn't score any runs. (4) .... they lost, their fans gave them a big round of applause.

D Although, even though, in spite of, and despite (1–4)

Join each pair of sentences. Be careful where you put the words in parentheses.

▶ Duncan used to smoke. He seems to be in good health. (although)
Although Duncan used to smoke, he seems to be in good health.

▶ I couldn't sleep. I was tired. (despite)
I couldn't sleep despite being tired.

1 Ethan didn't notice the sign. It was right in front of him. (even though)
....

2 Richard doesn't know any French. He studied it in high school. (although)
....

3 Henri's friend is a millionaire. He hates spending money. (despite)
....

4 We couldn't get tickets. We lined up for an hour. (in spite of)
....

E Whereas, on the other hand, in spite of, and although (4–5)

Put one of the linking words into each of these sentences.

▶ Although it was rush hour, the roads weren't at all busy.

1 I always spend money when I have it. My brother, ..., is very careful.

2 I managed to do some studying .... all the noise.

3 People are friendly out east, ... around here, no one speaks to you.

To, in order to, so that, and for

1 Introduction

We use **to, in order to, so that,** and **for** to express purpose, to say why we do things. The purpose of stopping is to buy a newspaper.

2 To

We can use the **to**-infinitive to express purpose.

*Vanessa was hurrying **to catch** her bus.* *Most people work **to earn** money.*
*I called **to find** out the train schedule.* *We went to the library **to get** some books.*

3 In order to and so as to

In order to and **so as to** are more formal than **to.**

*The government took these measures **in order to** reduce crime.*
*The employees are working on weekends **so as to** complete the project in time.*

We can use the negative **in order not to** or **so as not to.**

*Vanessa was hurrying **in order not to** miss her bus.*
*The employees are working on weekends **so as not to** delay the project any further.*

We cannot use **not to** on its own.

*She was hurrying **to catch** her bus.* NOT ~~*She was hurrying not to miss her bus.*~~

4 So that

Look at this example.

*I'll mail the card today **so that it gets** there on Xavier's birthday.*

After **so that** we use a subject and verb, e.g. **it gets.**

We often use **will** or **can** for a present purpose and **would** or **could** for a past purpose.

*I'll give you a map **so that** you **can** find/you**'ll** find the way around.*
*I gave Nikhil a map **so that** he **could** find/**would** be able to find the way around.*

5 To or for?

We can use **for** with a noun to say why we do something.

*The whole family have gone out **for** a bike ride.* *Why don't you come over **for** coffee?*

To talk about the purpose of a thing, we use either a **to**-infinitive or **for** + an **-ing** form.

*This heater is **to keep/for keeping** the plants warm in winter.*
*This machine is used **to cut/for cutting** plastic.*

But we do not use **for** + an **-ing** form to talk about a specific action.

*I put the heater on **to keep** the plants warm.* NOT ~~*I put the heater on for keeping the plants warm.*~~

Practice

A To (2)

Complete each sentence using *to* and these words:
~~cash a cheque~~*, *pay her tuition*, *go to sleep*, *hear the local news*, *look professional

▶ Hazel went to the bank to cash a cheque.
1 Doug sometimes takes a pill ....
2 Sue turned on the radio ....
3 Just this once, Randy is going to wear a suit ....
4 Jessica is borrowing some money ....

B In order to and so as to (3)

Claude wants to succeed in business, so he is listening to a lecture on the subject. Here is what the speaker is telling the audience.

	ACTION		PURPOSE
▶	study the market	→	be more successful
1	get to work earlier	→	impress the boss
2	work harder	→	achieve more
3	take risks	→	be a winner
4	think positively	→	not miss any opportunities

Say what Claude is going to do. Use either *in order to* or *so as to*. Both are correct.

▶ He's going to study the market in order to be more successful.
1 ....
2 ....
3 ....
4 ....

C To, for, and so that (2, 4, 5)

Comment on what each person says. Use the word in parentheses.

▶ Grace: I'm learning English. I want to get a better job. (to)
Grace is learning English to get a better job.

▶ Jeff: I study encyclopedias. Then I can answer trivia questions. (so that)
Jeff studies encyclopedias so that he can answer trivia questions.

▶ Vicky: I'm saving up. I'm planning a vacation. (for)
Vicky is saving up for a vacation.

1 Tanya: I keep a dog. It guards the house. (to)
....

2 David: I'm going to be very careful. Then I won't have an accident. (so that)
....

3 Jessica: I'm going on a diet. I want to lose weight. (to)
....

4 Marisol: I often turn off the heat. It saves money. (to)
....

5 Talia: I had to go to Montreal. I had a business meeting. (for)
....

6 Isabel: I wore boots because I didn't want my feet to get cold. (so that)
....

Review test

Choose the correct answer (a, b, c, d) and write a, b, c, or d, as in the example.
The correct answers are on page 128.

Verbs

1 I'm busy right now. .... on the computer.
a I work   b I'm work   c I'm working   d I working

2 My friend .... the answer to the question.
a is know   b know   c knowing   d knows

3 When I looked into the room, the baby .... quietly.
a is sleeping   b slept   c was sleeping   d were sleeping

4 We .... to Jasper for vacation last year.
a goes   b going   c have gone   d went

5 Robert .... sick for three weeks. He's still in the hospital.
a had been   b has been   c is   d was

6 I'm very tired. .... more than 500 kilometres today.
a I drive   b I'm driving   c I've been driving   d I've driven

7 Our friends .... meet us at the airport tonight.
a are   b are going to   c go to   d will be to

8 .... a party next Saturday. We've sent out the invitations.
a We had   b We have   c We'll have   d We're having

9 At this time tomorrow .... over the Atlantic.
a we flying   b we'll be flying   c we'll fly   d we to fly

Questions, negatives, and answers

10 What's the weather like in Iqaluit? How often .... there?
a does it snow   b does it snows   c snow it   d snows it

11 What did you leave the meeting early ....? ~ I didn't feel very well.
a away   b because   c for   d like

12 Unfortunately the driver .... the red light.
a didn't saw   b didn't see   c no saw   d saw not

Modal verbs

13 The pharmacy was open, so luckily I .... buy some medicine.
a can b can't c did can d was able to

14 Petra has to work very hard. I .... do her job, I'm sure.
a can't b couldn't c don't d shouldn't

15 I've lost the key. I ought .... it in a safe place.
a that I put b to be putting c to have put d to put

Passive

16 The story I've just read .... Margaret Atwood.
a was written b was written by c was written from d wrote

The infinitive and the -ing form

17 The driver was arrested for failing .... an accident.
a of report b report c reporting d to report

18 Someone suggested .... for a walk.
a go b going c of going d to go

19 The police want .... anything suspicious.
a that we report b us reporting c us to report d we report

20 We weren't sure .... or just walk in.
a should knock b to knock c whether knock d whether to knock

21 It was too cold .... outside.
a the guests eating b for the guests to eat c that the guests should eat d that the guests eat

22 As we walked past, we saw Nigel .... his car.
a in washing b to wash c wash d washing

Nouns and articles (a/an and the)

23 I was watching TV at home when suddenly .... rang.
a a doorbell b an doorbell c doorbell d the doorbell

24 I've always liked ....
a Chinese food b food of China c some food of China d the Chinese food

Pronouns

25 Everyone in the group shook hands with ....
a each other b one other c one the other d themselves

26 All the guests were dancing. .... having a good time.
a All were b Every was c Everyone was d Someone were

Adjectives and adverbs

27 The young man seems very ....
a sensible b sensiblely c sensibley d sensibly

28 Yes, I received the report. .... it.
a I just am reading b I'm just reading c I'm reading just d Just I'm reading

Prepositions

29 The town is .... Edmonton. It's only ten kilometres away.
a along b by c near d next

30 We've lived in this apartment .... five years.
a ago b already c for d since

Verbs with prepositions and adverbs

31 I prefer dogs .... cats. I hate cats.
a from b over c than d to

32 My father used the money he won to set .... his own company.
a forward b on c out d up

Reported speech

33 Last week Justin said "I'll do it tomorrow." He said he would do it ....
a the following day b the previous day c tomorrow d yesterday

34 I don't know why Nancy didn't go to the meeting. She said she .... definitely going.
a be b is c was d would

35 The librarian asked us .... so much noise.
a don't make b not make c not making d not to make

Relative clauses

36 What's the name of the man .... gave us a lift?
a he b what c which d who

37 Susan is the woman .... husband is in hospital.
a her b hers the c whose d whose the

Conditionals and **wish**

38 If .... my passport, I'll be in trouble.
a I lose b I'll lose c I lost d I would lose

39 I don't have a ticket. If .... one, I could get in.
a I'd have b I had c I have d I've got

40 If the bus to the airport hadn't been so late, we .... the plane.
a caught b had caught c would catch d would have caught

Linking words

41 I just had to take the dog out .... of the awful weather.
a although b despite c even though d in spite

42 Anna put the heat on .... warm.
a for getting b in order get c so she gets d to get

Appendix 1: Word formation

A Introduction

Look at these examples.

*Lots of people believe that God **exists**.*

*Lots of people believe in the **existence** of God.*

Exist is a verb and **existence** is a noun. The word **existence** has two parts: **exist-** and **-ence**. We call **-ence** a "suffix." We add it to the end of the verb **exist** to form a noun.

We can also use suffixes to form verbs, adjectives, and adverbs.

*The system is being **modernized**. (= made modern)*

*I grew up in an **industrial** town. (= a town where there is a lot of industry)*

*The man was behaving **strangely**. (= in a strange way)*

There are many different suffixes, such as **-ence**, **-ize**, **-al**, **-ly**, **-tion**, and **-ment**. Some of them can be used to form many different words. For example, there are a lot of nouns ending in **-tion: action, education, explanation, information, instruction**, etc. There are no exact rules about which suffix you can add to which word. Adding a suffix can also involve other changes to the form of a word.

industry → industrial   repeat → repetition   science → scientist

Now look at these examples.

*They're going to **play** the game on Wednesday.*

*They're going to **replay** the game on Wednesday.*

We can add **re-** to the beginning of the verb **play**. We call **re-** a "prefix." A prefix adds something to the meaning of a word. The verb **replay** means "play again." We can also add prefixes to nouns and adjectives. See parts G and H.

B Noun suffixes

-ment	*the prospects for **employment*** *reach an **agreement***
-ion/-tion/-sion	*take part in a **discussion*** *increase steel **production*** *ask for **permission***
-ation/-ition	*an **invitation** to a party* *people's **opposition** to the idea*
-ence/-ance	*a **preference** for houses rather than condos* *a **distance** of ten kilometres*
-ty/-ity	*no **certainty** that we shall succeed* *keep the door locked for **security***
-ness	*people's **willingness** to help* *recovering from an **illness***
-ing	*enter a **building*** *reach an **understanding***

C Nouns for people

-er/-or	*the **driver** of the car* *a newspaper **editor***
-ist	*a place full of **tourists*** *a **scientist** doing an experiment*
-ant/-ent	*an **assistant** to help with my work* ***students** at the university*
-an/-ian	***Republicans** and Democrats* *the **electrician** rewiring the house*
-ee	*an **employee** of the company (= someone employed)* *notes for **trainees** (= people being trained)*

We also use **-er** for things, especially machines.

*a hair **dryer***   *a food **mixer***   *a **blender***

D Verb suffixes

Many verbs are formed by adding **-ize** or **-ise** to an adjective. Some are formed by adding **-en**.

-ize	*European safety rules are being **standardized**.* *They **privatized** the company.*
-en	*They're going to **widen** the road here.* *I think this will **brighten** her day.*

E Adjective suffixes

Most of these adjectives are formed from nouns.

-al	*a **professional** musician Canada's **coastal** waters*
-ic	*a **metallic** sound a **scientific** inquiry*
-ive	*an **informative** guidebook an offer **exclusive** to our readers*
-ful	*a **successful** career feeling **hopeful** about the future*
-less	*feeling **hopeless** about the future (= without hope) **powerless** to do anything about it*
-ous	*guilty of **dangerous** driving **luxurious** vacation homes*
-y	*a **rocky** path the **salty** taste of sea water*
-ly	*a **friendly** smile a very **lively** person*
-able/-ible	*an **acceptable** error (= an error that can be accepted) a **comprehensible** explanation a **valuable** painting (= worth a lot of money) a **comfortable** chair*

F Adverbs

-ly	*He looked around **nervously**. I moved here very **recently**.*

G Some common prefixes

anti- (= against)	***anti-whaling** protestors **anti-government** troops*
inter- (= between)	*an **international** match **interstate** highways in the US*
mini- (= small)	*a **miniskirt** the **minibar** in your hotel room*
mis- (= wrongly)	***mishear** what someone says **miscalculate** the amount*
multi- (= many)	***multicoloured** lights a **multimillionaire***
over- (= too much)	*a tendency to **overeat** **overcrowded** roads*
post- (= after)	*the **post-war** world a **postgraduate** student*
pre- (= before)	***pre-game** entertainment in **prehistoric** times*
re- (= again)	*a **reunion** of old friends **reread** a favourite book*
semi- (= half)	***semi-skilled** work sitting in a **semicircle***
super- (= big)	*a huge new **superstore** a **supertanker** carrying oil*
under- (= too little)	*thin and **underweight** **underpaid** work*

H Negative prefixes

We can also use a prefix to form an opposite. For example, the opposite of **clear** is **unclear** (= not clear). **Un-** is the most common negative prefix.

dis-	*a **dishonest** way to behave can't help being **disorganized** **dislike** the idea **disappear** from the scene a **disadvantage** of the plan*
il- (+ **l**)	*an **illegal** drug an **illogical** answer*
im- (+ **m** or **p**)	*an **impossible** task an **impolite** question*
in-	*an **indirect** route the **invisible** man a great **injustice***
ir- (+ **r**)	*an **irregular** shape an **irrelevant** remark*
non-	***non-alcoholic** drinks a **non-stop** flight*
un-	*an **uncomfortable** chair an **unusual** event an **undated** letter **uncertain** what to do **unpack** your suitcase **unzip** the bag*

Appendix 2: The spelling of endings

A Plural nouns

We add **-s** to a noun to form the plural.

a car → *two cars*   *a name* → *some names*

1 After **-s**, **-sh**, **-ch**, and **-x** we add **-es** /ɪz/.

glass → *glass**es***   *dish* → *dish**es***
match → *match**es***   *box* → *box**es***

2 A few nouns ending in **-o** have **-es**.

*hero**es***   *potato**es***   *tomato**es***
But most have **s**.
*kilo**s***   *photo**s***   *piano**s***
*stereo**s***   *studio**s***   *zoo**s***

3 When a noun ends in a consonant + **-y**, the **-y** changes to **-ies**.

*penn**y*** → *penn**ies***   *stor**y*** → *stor**ies***
We do not change **-y** after a vowel.
*da**y*** → *da**ys***   *alle**y*** → *alle**ys***

B The Simple Present -s ending

In the third person singular, a Simple Present verb ends in **-s**.

I know → *he know**s***   *I work* → *she work**s***

1 After **-s**, **-sh**, **-ch** and **-x** we add **-es** /ɪz/.

pass → *pass**es***   *wash* → *wash**es***
catch → *catch**es***   *mix* → *mix**es***

2 Some verbs ending in **-o** have **-es**.

go → *go**es*** /ɡəʊz/   *do* → *do**es*** /dʌz/

3 When a verb ends in a consonant + **-y**, the **-y** changes to **-ies**.

*hurr**y*** → *hurr**ies***   *cop**y*** → *cop**ies***
We do not change **-y** after a vowel.
*sta**y*** → *sta**ys***   *enjo**y*** → *enjo**ys***

C The -ed ending

Most verbs have **-ed** in the past tense. Most past participles also end in **-ed**.

look → *look**ed***   *call* → *call**ed***

1 If the verb ends in **-e**, we add **-d**.

hope → *hope**d***   *save* → *save**d***

2 When a verb ends in a consonant + **-y**, the **-y** changes to **-ied**.

*hurr**y*** → *hurr**ied***   *cop**y*** → *cop**ied***

3 Sometimes we double a final consonant. This happens when a one-syllable verb ends with one vowel and one consonant, e.g. *b**eg**, pl**an***.

*b**eg*** → *be**gg**ed*   *pl**an*** → *pla**nn**ed*
For more details about doubling, see part G.

D The -ing form

1 We normally leave out **-e** when we add **-ing** to a verb.

*tak**e*** → *tak**ing***   *driv**e*** → *driv**ing***
But we keep a double **e** before **-ing**.
*s**ee*** → *s**ee**ing*   *agr**ee*** → *agr**ee**ing*

2 When a verb ends in **-ie**, it changes to **-ying**.

*d**ie*** → *d**ying***   *l**ie*** → *l**ying***
But **-y** does not change.
*hurr**y*** → *hurr**ying***

3 Sometimes we double a final consonant. This happens when a one-syllable verb ends with one vowel and one consonant, e.g. *w**in**, p**ut***.

*w**in*** → *wi**nn**ing*   *p**ut*** → *pu**tt**ing*
For more details about doubling, see part G.

E Adverbs

We form many adverbs from an adjective + **-ly**.

slow → *slow**ly***   *calm* → *calm**ly***

1 We do not leave out **-e** before **-ly**.

*saf**e*** → *saf**ely***   *strang**e*** → *strang**ely***
But there are a few exceptions.
due → *duly*   *true* → *truly*
whole → *wholly*

2 When an adjective ends in a consonant + **-y**, the **-y** changes to **-ily**.

*angr**y*** → *angr**ily***   *happ**y*** → *happ**ily***
An exception is *shy* → *shyly.*

3 When an adjective ends in a consonant + **-le**, the **-e** changes to **-y**.

*proba**ble*** → *proba**bly***   *sensi**ble*** → *sensi**bly***

4 When an adjective ends in **-ic**, we add **-ally**.

automatic → *automatic**ally*** /ɔːtəˈmætɪkli/
romantic → *romantic**ally*** /rəʊˈmæntɪkli/
But there is one exception.
public → *publicly*

F The comparison of adjectives

We form the comparative and superlative of short adjectives with **-er** and **-est**.

old → *old**er**, old**est***
quick → *quick**er**, quick**est***

1 If the adjective ends in **-e**, we add **-r** and **-st**.
late → *late**r**, late**st*** *fine* → *fine**r**, fine**st***

2 When an adjective ends in a consonant + **-y**, the **-y** changes to **-ier** or **-iest**.
*heav**y*** → *heav**ier**, heav**iest***
*luck**y*** → *luck**ier**, luck**iest***

3 Sometimes we double a final consonant. This happens when a one-syllable adjective ends with one vowel and one consonant, e.g. ***big**, **flat**.*
big → *bi**gg**er, bi**gg**est* *flat* → *fla**tt**er, fla**tt**est*
For more details about doubling, see part G.

G The doubling of consonants

1 When we add **-ed**, **-ing**, **-er**, or **-est** to a word, we sometimes double a final consonant. This happens when a one-syllable word ends with one vowel and one consonant, e.g. ***stop**, **get**, **thin**, **sad**.*
*sto**p*** → *sto**pp**ed* *ge**t*** → *ge**tt**ing*
*thi**n*** → *thi**nn**er* *sa**d*** → *sa**dd**est*

2 We do not double **-y**, **-w**, or **-x**.
play → *played* *new* → *newest*
fax → *faxing*
We do not double when there are two consonants.
*a**sk*** → *asking* *sho**rt*** → *shortest*
*ri**ch*** → *richer*
And we do not double when there are two vowels.
*s**ee**m* → *seemed* *sh**ou**t* → *shouting*
*f**ai**r* → *fairest*

3 The rule about doubling is also true for words of more than one syllable (e.g. *permit = per + mit*), but only if the last syllable is stressed.
per'mit → *per'mi**tt**ed*
pre'fer → *pre'fe**rr**ing*
We do not usually double a consonant when the syllable is unstressed.
'open → *opened* *'enter* → *entering*
An exception is that in Canadian English **-l** is usually doubled, even if the syllable is unstressed.
travel → *trave**ll**ed*

Appendix 3: Punctuation

A Period (.), question mark (?), and exclamation mark (!)

A sentence ends with one of these punctuation marks.

Period:	*It's cold today.*	*The office was closed.*	*Please be careful.*
Question mark:	*Who's that?*	*Did you see the show?*	*Could you wait, please?*
Exclamation mark:	*Oh, no! I don't believe it!*		

B Semi-colon (;)

We can use a semi-colon between two separate statements which are linked in meaning.

Jenna is a very kind person; she visits Sri in the hospital every day.

We could also use a period here.

C Colon (:)

We can use a colon before an explanation or before a list.

Vicky felt nervous: she hated the dark.

There wasn't much in the fridge: a couple of sausages, some butter, and half a bottle of milk.

D Dash (–)

A dash is informal. It is sometimes used instead of a colon or a semi-colon.

I'm having a great time—there's a lot to do here.

Marisol felt nervous—she hated the dark.

E Comma (,)

We often use a comma when we link two statements with **and**, **but**, or **or**.

Daniel was tired, and his feet were hurting. *It's a really good camera, but I can't afford it.*

Note the two subjects in each sentence: *Daniel... his feet* and *It... I.* When there is only one subject, we do not use a comma.

Daniel sat down and took his shoes off.

We can also use a comma when a sentence has a linking word like **when** or **although**.

When the office is busy, Marina has to work late.

Sometimes a comma can separate an adverb or a phrase.

Marina, unfortunately, has to work late. *On busy days, Marina has to work late.*

Here the commas separate *unfortunately* and *on busy days.*

The rules about commas are not very exact. In general, commas are more likely around longer phrases. With a short phrase there is often no comma.

On busy days Marina has to work late. *Sometimes she has to work late.*

It is less usual to separate something at the end of the sentence.

Marina has to work late when the office is busy. *She stayed late to get the work done.*

We do not usually put a comma before **to** expressing purpose.

We also use commas in a list of more than two. The last two are linked by **and**, often without a comma.

I went out with Rachel, Vicky, Emma, and Matthew. (Or *I went out with Rachel, Vicky, Emma and Matthew.*)

F Quotation marks (“ ”)

We put direct speech in quotation marks.

Tatiana said, “You haven't put those shelves up yet.” *“I haven't had time,” replied Nikhil.*

We normally use a comma to separate the direct speech from the rest of the sentence. The comma comes before the quotation mark. Quotation marks are also called “quotes.”

Single quotation marks are sometimes used.

Tatiana said, ‘You haven't put those shelves up yet.’

We can put quotation marks around titles.

Have you read the poem “The Divine Comedy”?

We often use quotation marks when we mention a word or phrase.

What does “punctuation” mean? *She calls her work “performance art.”*

G Hyphen (-)

We sometimes use hyphens in these structures.

Compound noun: *a six-pack of pop*
Compound expression before a noun: *an oven-ready meal*
Noun formed from a phrasal verb: *ready for take-off*
Noun + **-ing** form: *interested in rock-climbing*
Before the last word of a compound number: *a hundred and twenty-six people*
After some prefixes: *anti-aircraft guns*

The rules about hyphens are not very exact. For example, you may see a compound noun written as **phonecard, phone-card** or **phone card.** Hyphens are not very frequent in Canadian English. If you are unsure, it is usually safer to write two separate words.

H Apostrophe (')

Look at these examples.

Today we're going up to the cottage. *Everyone is looking at Wilmer's car.*

We use an apostrophe (') in short forms, when there is a missing letter, e.g. **we're** (= we are). We also use an apostrophe with **s** to form the possessive of a noun, e.g. **Wilmer's car.**

I Capital letters

There are two capital letters (big letters) in this sentence.

*The boss said **I** could leave early.*

We use a capital letter at the beginning of a sentence and for the word **I.**

We also use a capital letter to begin the names of people, places, companies, etc.

Mark and Sarah *Quebec City* *Main Street* *Parliament Hill* *Research in Motion*

This includes the names of books, movies, magazines, etc. All the important words start with a capital letter.

A Fine Balance *Away from Her* *Macleans*

We also use a capital letter for days of the week, months of the year, holidays and festivals, historical times, nationalities, and most abbreviations.

Monday *August* *Easter* *the New Year* *the Industrial Revolution*
some Italian wine *the UN* (= the United Nations)

Appendix 4: Pronunciation

A Key to phonetic symbols

VOWELS

iː	feed	ʌ	cup
i	happy	ɜː	bird
ɪ	sit	ə	away
e	ten	ei	pay
æ	sad	əʊ	so
ɑː	car	ai	cry
ɒ	dog	au	now
ɔː	ball	ɔɪ	boy
ʊ	put	ə	dear
u	actual	eə	chair
uː	fool	ʊə	sure

CONSONANTS

p	put	f	first	h	house
b	best	v	van	m	must
t	tell	θ	three	n	next
d	day	ð	this	ŋ	song
k	cat	s	sell	l	love
g	good	z	zoo	r	rest
tʃ	cheese	ʃ	ship	j	you
dʒ	just	ʒ	vision	w	will

B Stress

In books about English, the symbol ' is used before a stressed syllable, the part of the word which is spoken with greater force.

midnight /'mɪdnaɪt/ *about* /ə'baʊt/ *exercise* /'eksəsaɪz/ *belonging* /bɪ'lɒŋɪŋ/

Here the syllables **mid**, **bout**, **ex**, and **long** are stressed. It is important to get the stress on the correct part of the word. Stressing a word incorrectly can make it difficult to understand.

Now look at these two sentences.

We want to **protest** /prə'test/ *against experiments on live animals.*

We want to organize a **protest** /'prəʊtest/ *against experiments on live animals.*

Protest as a verb is stressed on the second syllable. As a noun it is stressed on the first syllable. There are a number of words like this, e.g. **conflict**, **contrast**, **export**, **import**, **increase**, **insult**, **produce**, **progress**, **protest**, **record**, **suspect**, **transfer**. Sometimes a change of stress means a change of vowel sound.

Verbs: *produce* /prə'djuːs/, *progress* /prə'gres/, *record* /rɪ'kɔːd/

Nouns: *produce* /'prɒdjuːs/, *progress* /'prəʊgres/, *record* /'rekɔːd/

We also use stress to show which are the important words in a sentence.

'Claire has a 'lovely 'house. She 'bought it last 'year. It's 'right in the 'centre of 'town.

Here the important words are **Claire**, **lovely**, **house**, and so on. We do not usually stress "grammatical words" like **a**, **she**, **the**, and **of**.

C Intonation

The voice usually falls or rises on the most important word in the sentence. This word is usually at or near the end of the sentence.

Claire has a lovely ↘ *house.*

Here the voice falls when saying **house**, which is the key word.

The symbol ↘ is used for a falling intonation and ↗ for a rising intonation.

Everything is more or less ↘ *ready.* (a statement)

Everything is more or less ↗ *ready?* (a question)

The voice usually goes down in a statement and up in a yes/no question. In general, a fall means that what we say is complete. A rise means that what we say is incomplete, or it needs an answer.

The voice often rises in the first part of a sentence and falls at the end.

If you don't ↗ mind, I ought to be ↘ going.

There is always a fall or rise on the important part of the message. Which word is the key word depends on the meaning. Compare these examples.

My friend is upset. She just failed her ↘ exam.
I passed my exam last summer, but my friend has just ↘ failed hers.
Lots of people have failed their exams. My ↘ friend just failed hers.

D Voicing

Sounds can be voiced or voiceless. Voiced sounds are like those you make when you sing. All the vowels and some of the consonants are voiced.Voiceless sounds are like those you make when you whisper. Some of the consonants are voiceless. Compare these sounds.

VOICED		VOICELESS	
/b/	***bill***	/p/	***pill***
/d/	***down***	/t/	***town***
/g/	***gold***	/k/	***cold***
/z/	***prize***	/s/	***price***

The voiceless sounds are /p/, /t/, /k/, /f/, /θ/, /s/, /ʃ/, /tʃ/, and /h/.

E The -s ending

We sometimes add the ending **-s** or **-es** to a word. For example, we can do this to form the plural or the possessive of a noun.

*some chair**s***   *the bush**es***   *Mark**'s** car*   *the woman**'s** name*

We can also add **-s** or **-es** to a verb.

*It look**s** nice and sunny.*   *Eric watch**es** football on Sunday afternoons.*

The pronunciation of **-s/-es** depends on the sound which is before it. The ending is pronounced /s/ after a voiceless sound, /z/ after a voiced sound, and /ɪz/ after a sibilant sound.

Voiceless + /s/	***lips*** /ps/	***gets*** /ts/	***takes*** /ks/
Voiced + /z/	***jobs*** /bz/	***hides*** /dz/	***bags*** /gz/
	Laura's /əz/	***days*** /eɪz/	***knows*** /əʊz/
Sibilant + /ɪz/	***buses*** /sɪz/	***loses*** /zɪz/	***crashes*** /ʃɪz/

For voiced and voiceless sounds see part D. The sibilant sounds are /s/, /z/, /ʃ/, /ʒ/, /tʃ/, and /dʒ/.

F The -ed ending

We add **-ed** or **-d** to a regular verb to form the past tense or past participle.

*We all **walked** home.*   *They've **closed** the gates.*

The pronunciation of **-ed** depends on the sound coming before it. The ending is pronounced /t/ after a voiceless sound, /d/ after a voiced sound, and /ɪd/ after /t/ or /d/.

Voiceless + /t/	***hoped*** /pt/	***worked*** /kt/	***increased*** /st/
Voiced + /d/	***robbed*** /bd/	***begged*** /gd/	***raised*** /zd/
	played /eɪd/	***allowed*** /aʊd/	***cared*** /eəd/
/t/ or /d/ + /ɪd/	***wanted*** /tɪd/	***landed*** /dɪd/	

For voiced and voiceless sounds see part D.

G Weak forms

We are using a weak form when we pronounce **is** as /s/ rather than /ɪz/, or we pronounce **from** as /frəm/ rather than /frɒm/. Normally a word like **is** or **from** is not stressed, and so we can use a weak form.

	STRONG FORM	WEAK FORM		STRONG FORM	WEAK FORM
a	/eɪ/	/ə/	*is*	/ɪz/	/z/ or /s/
am	/æm/	/əm/ or /m/	*me*	/miː/	/mi/
an	/æn/	/ən/	*must*	/mʌst/	/məst/ or /məs/
and	/ænd/	/ənd/, /ən/ or /n/	*of*	/ɒv/	/əv/ or /v/
are	/ɑː(r)/	/ə(r)/	*shall*	/ʃæl/	/ʃəl/ or /ʃl/
as	/æz/	/əz/	*she*	/ʃiː/	/ʃi/
at	/æt/	/ət/	*should*	/ʃʊd/	/ʃəd/
be	/biː/	/bi/	*some*	/sʌm/	/səm/ or /sm/
been	/biːn/	/bɪn/	*than*	/ðæn/	/ðən/
can	/kæn/	/kən/	*that*	/ðæt/	/ðət/
could	/kʊd/	/kəd/	*the*	/ðiː/	/ði/ or /ðə/
do	/duː/	/du/ or /də/	*them*	/ðem/	/ðəm/ or /əm/
for	/fɔː(r)/	/fə(r)/	*there*	/ðeə(r)/	/ðə(r)/
from	/frɔm/	/frəm/	*to*	/tuː/	/tu/ or /tə/
had	/hæd/	/həd/, /əd/ or /d/	*was*	/wɒz/	/wəz/
has	/hæz/	/həz/, /əz/ or /z/	*we*	/wiː/	/wi/
have	/hæv/	/həv/, /əv/ or /v/	*were*	/wɜː(r)/	/wə(r)/
he	/hiː/	/hi/ or /i/	*will*	/wɪl/	/l/
her	/hɜː(r)/	/hə(r)/ or /ə(r)/	*would*	/wʊd/	/wəd/, /əd/ or /d/
him	/hɪm/	/ɪm/	*you*	/juː/	/ju/
his	/hɪz/	/ɪz/	*your*	/jɔː(r)/	/jə(r)/

Notes on weak forms

1 (r) means that an -r sound is pronounced before a vowel. In the phrase **for a minute**, the words **for a** are pronounced /fəre/.

2 **A, an,** and **the** are normally spoken in their weak form.

3 **Some** does not have a weak form when it means "some but not all."

4 **That** normally has a weak form when it is a linking word, e.g. *I knew **that** /ðət/ it was true.* It does not have a weak form when it means something at a distance from the speaker, e.g. *Look at **that** /ðæt/ car.*

5 **There** normally has a weak form in a sentence like ***There's** /ðəz/ a bookstore in town.*
It does not have a weak form when it means "in that place," e.g. *The bookstore is over **there** /ðeə/.*

6 A verb does not have a weak form in a short answer with **yes**.
*Are you tired? ~ Yes, **I am** /æm/.*

Appendix 5: Irregular verbs

VERB	PAST TENSE	PAST/PASSIVE PARTICIPLE
arise	arose	arisen
be	was, were	been
bear	bore	borne
beat	beat	beaten
become	became	become
begin	began	begun
bend	bent	bent
bet	bet	bet
		betted
bind	bound	bound
bite	bit	bitten
		bit
bleed	bled	bled
blow	blew	blown
break	broke	broken
breed	bred	bred
bring	brought	brought
broadcast	broadcast	broadcast
build	built	built
burn	burned	burned
	burnt	burnt
burst	burst	burst
buy	bought	bought
catch	caught	caught
choose	chose	chosen
come	came	come
cost	cost	cost
creep	crept	crept
cut	cut	cut
deal /diːl/	dealt /delt/	dealt /delt/
dig	dug	dug
dive	dove	dived
	dived	
do	did	done
draw	drew	drawn
dream	dreamed	dreamed
/driːm/	dreamt	dreamt
	/dremt/	/dremt/
drink	drank	drunk
drive	drove	driven
eat /iːt/	ate /et/	eaten /ˈiːtn/
fall	fell	fallen
feed	fed	fed
feel	felt	felt
fight	fought	fought
find	found	found
flee	fled	fled
fly	flew	flown
forbid	forbad(e)	forbidden
	/fəˈbæd/	
forget	forgot	forgotten
forgive	forgave	forgiven
freeze	froze	frozen
get	got	gotten
give	gave	given
go	went	gone
grind	ground	ground
grow	grew	grown
hang	hung	hung
have	had	had
hear /hɪə/	heard /hɜːd/	heard /hɜːd/
hide	hid	hidden
hit	hit	hit
hold	held	held
hurt	hurt	hurt
keep	kept	kept
kneel	knelt	knelt
know	knew	known
lay	laid	laid
lead	led	led
lean /liːn/	leaned	leaned
leap /liːp/	leapt /lept/	leapt /lept/
	leaped	leaped
learn	learned	learned
leave	left	left
lend	lent	lent
let	let	let
lie	lay	lain
light	lit	lit
	lighted	lighted
lose	lost	lost
make	made	made
mean /miːn/	meant /ment/	meant /ment/
meet	met	met
mow	mowed	mown
		mowed

VERB	PAST TENSE	PAST/PASSIVE PARTICIPLE
pay	paid	paid
put	put	put
read /riːd/	read /red/	read /red/
ride	rode	ridden
ring	rang	rung
rise	rose	risen
run	ran	run
say /seɪ/	said /sed/	said /sed/
see	saw	seen
seek	sought	sought
sell	sold	sold
send	sent	sent
set	set	set
sew	sewed	sewn
		sewed
shake	shook	shaken
shine	shone	shone
shoot	shot	shot
show	showed	shown
shrink	shrank	shrunk
	shrunk	
shut	shut	shut
sing	sang	sung
sink	sank	sunk
sit	sat	sat
sleep	slept	slept
slide	slid	slid
smell	smelled	smelled
speak	spoke	spoken
speed	sped	sped
	speeded	speeded
spell	spelled	spelled
spend	spent	spent
spill	spilled	spilled
	spilt	spilt
spin	spun	spun
spit	spat	spat
split	split	split
spoil	spoiled	spoiled
spread	spread	spread
spring	sprang	sprung

VERB	PAST TENSE	PAST/PASSIVE PARTICIPLE
stand	stood	stood
steal	stole	stolen
stick	stuck	stuck
sting	stung	stung
stink	stank	stunk
	stunk	
stride	strode	stridden
strike	struck	struck
swear	swore	sworn
sweep	swept	swept
swim	swam	swum
swing	swung	swung
take	took	taken
teach	taught	taught
tear	tore	torn
tell	told	told
think	thought	thought
throw	threw	thrown
tread	trod	trodden
understand	understood	understood
wake	woke	woken
	waked	waked
wear	wore	worn
weave	wove	woven
	weaved	weaved
weep	wept	wept
win	won	won
wind	wound	wound
write	wrote	written

The verbs in this list are also irregular when they have a prefix, e.g. **overtake – overtook – overtaken, foretell – foretold – foretold.**

A few verbs have irregular Simple Present forms:

VERB	SIMPLE PRESENT
be	I **am**; you/we/they **are**; he/she/it **is**
do	he/she/it **does** /dʌz/
go	he/she/it **goes** /gəʊz/
have	he/she/it **has**
say	he/she/it **says** /sez/

Answer key

Pages 2–3

A
1. He's/He is talking
2. I think
3. they're/they are discussing
4. Are you looking
5. Do you know
6. works
7. She doesn't work
8. You know
9. I give
10. she gives
11. She lives
12. It saves
13. I agree
14. I'm/I am wasting

B
1. It's/It is snowing, It's/It is coming
2. I start, I'm/I am starting
3. I'm/I am going, I drive
4. rises, we're/we are travelling
5. I'm/I am writing, I promise
6. I want, I'm/I am saving

C
1. she always takes
2. She's/She is always missing
3. do you always go
4. They're/They are always arguing.

Pages 4–5

A
1. He sat down on a chair while I was painting it.
2. As he was running for a bus, he collided with a lamppost.
3. His hair caught fire when he was frying onion rings.
4. When he was holding a beautiful vase, he suddenly dropped it.
5. He was sitting in the backyard when a bee stung him on the nose.

B
1. We lost
2. it came
3. was coming
4. went
5. fell
6. were playing
7. I was working
8. I lost
9. I got
10. did

C
1. The train was waiting when we arrived at the station.
2. I was reading a library book when I found a ten-dollar bill in it.
3. Arianna got an electric shock when she touched the wire.
4. When the doors opened, the crowd rushed in.
5. When the campers woke, they saw that the sun was shining.

Pages 6–7

A
1. have arrived
2. fixed
3. I've/I have lost
4. has started
5. ran
6. earned
7. We planted
8. have gone
9. has turned
10. I called
11. I've/I have made
12. broke

B
1. The bus drivers have gone on strike. They stopped work(ing) at twelve o'clock.
2. The Governor General has arrived in Toronto. He/She flew there in a helicopter.
3. Two men have escaped from Kingston Penitentiary. They got away during the night.
4. The author Yann Martel has written a new book. It came out last week.
5. Sharon Cherop has won the women's marathon. She ran it in 2 hours 22 minutes.

C
1. haven't taken a photo since
2. weeks since I last saw
3. was the last time we played
4. haven't eaten anything for

Pages 8–9

A
1. has stood
2. was
3. drank
4. 've/have lived
5. 've/have known
6. were

B
1. b
2. b
3. a

C
1. this, last
2. today, yesterday
3. last, this
4. this, yesterday

D
1. What's/What has happened OR What happened
2. He's/He has had OR He had
3. He fell
4. broke
5. did it happen
6. told
7. You have known
8. you didn't tell
9. I didn't see
10. I haven't seen
11. He's/He has had
12. He did

Pages 10–11

A
1. 's/has left, He's/He has been cleaning, he's/he has finished
2. I've/I have been working, You've/You have done
3. I've/I have heard, have you been doing, We've/We have done

B
1. How many kilometres have you walked?
2. How long have they been digging up the road?
3. How many photos have you taken?
4. How long has it been snowing?

C
1. I've/I have been cleaning
2. I've/I have found
3. You've/You have been sitting
4. I've/I have been watching
5. You've/You have been
6. I've/I have had
7. They've/They have been
8. I've/I have never had

Pages 12–13

A
1. 's/is going to read
2. 'll have
3. 'll record
4. are you going to buy

B
1. It's/It is going to attack us/me.
2. aliens will land on Earth in the next ten years.
3. she's/she is going to get married.
4. I'll invite her out for dinner.

C
1. We're/We are going to build
2. will be (OR is going to be)
3. will like (OR are going to like)
4. will be (OR are going to be)
5. We aren't going to cut (OR We won't cut)
6. We're/We are going to have
7. will be OR is going to be
8. We're/We are going to stop OR We will stop

Pages 14–15

A
1. future
2. future
3. present
4. future
5. present

B 1 She's/She is working on Saturday.
2 She's/She is flying to Cairo on May 15.
3 He's/He is seeing his boss at four o'clock this afternoon.
4 They're/They are playing tennis tomorrow afternoon.

C 1 I'm/I am going
2 He's/He is staying
3 gets
4 are you doing
5 I'm/I am going
6 finishes
7 we're/we are going

D 1 's/is about to win
2 are to go
3 is to visit
4 're/are about to move
5 are to take

Pages 16–17

A 1 I'll/I will be earning
2 I'll/I will be doing
3 will you be doing
4 I'll/I will be hosting
5 who'll/who will be doing
6 you'll/you will be playing

B 1 I'll/I will be seeing her
2 I'll/I will be going there next summer
3 I'll/I will be playing (it/badminton) next weekend.
4 I'll/I will be having lunch/it in the cafeteria tomorrow. OR I'll/I will be having lunch/it there tomorrow.

C 1 Will you be going to the library today?
2 Will you be writing to Alyssa soon?
3 Will you be using your calculator this afternoon?
4 Will you be seeing Daniel tomorrow?
5 Will you be driving to the concert?
6 Will you be calling your sister soon?

Pages 18–19

A 1 It's a difficult problem.
2 I've seen the results.
3 I don't have any information.
4 We haven't reached a decision.
5 I'm very excited about it.
6 You don't need to decide now.
7 It isn't yet certain. OR It's not yet certain.
8 We'll be happy to see you.
9 Don't worry.
10 I'd like to buy a new computer.
11 We're willing to help.
12 We won't know the result for some time.

B 1 Where's, It's
2 don't, isn't OR 's not
3 What's, He's

C 1 I would like a coffee, please.
2 There has been an accident.
3 That is correct.
4 I had seen the movie before.
5 Who has got the key?
6 We would have stopped if we had seen you.

Pages 20–21

A 1 What's/What is the date (today)?
2 When does the class end?
3 Who did you invite/have you invited (to your party)?
4 How can I/we get tickets (to the concert)?
5 Where are we going to have lunch? OR Where should we have lunch?

B 1 Where
2 How many
3 When
4 Who
5 What
6 How far
7 How often
8 What kind
9 How long

C 1 where do you tape
2 How many episodes have you done?
3 How much money do you earn?
4 When did you start acting?
5 What are your plans for the future?

Pages 22–23

A 1 What are you looking at?
2 What are you talking about?
3 What are you waiting for?
4 What are you pointing at?

B 1 What are you ashamed of?
2 What is she famous for?
3 What is he going to complain about?
4 What is she going to be late for?
5 What do you feel nervous about?

C 1 What
2 for
3 What
4 like
5 what
6 for
7 What
8 like
9 how

Pages 24–25

A 1 wasn't
2 had
3 don't know
4 didn't land
5 aren't sure
6 lived

B 1 can't
2 doesn't
3 didn't
4 weren't
5 wasn't
6 isn't
7 don't
8 haven't

C 1 doesn't get headaches.
2 can't relax.
3 didn't miss a lecture.
4 isn't a nervous person.
5 doesn't lose things.
6 wasn't a happy child.
7 hasn't decided on a career.

D 1 no
2 no
3 not
4 no
5 No
6 not

Pages 26–27

A 1 She can't play the violin.
2 He can climb trees.
3 She can juggle.
4 They can't lift the weights.

B 1 I can walk OR I'm able to walk
2 I can go OR I'll be able to go
3 to be able to get
4 been able to do

C 1 c
2 a

D 1 was able to
2 could
3 could/was able to
4 were able to
5 couldn't/wasn't able to

Pages 28–29

A (May and might are both possible.)
1 she might be
2 She may be
3 She might be sitting
4 She may be having
5 You might find
6 She might know

B 1 He may/might win.
2 I may/might take one.
3 We may/might get one.
4 She may/might be late.
5 They may/might be visiting me.

C 1 might not
2 might not
3 could not
4 could not
5 might not

D 1 can't
2 must
3 might
4 can't
5 might
6 must

Pages 30–31

A 1 shouldn't
2 ought
3 should
4 shouldn't
5 should
6 ought not

B 1 We'd better wait (for Clara).
2 You'd better lock it/ lock your bike.
3 I'd better clean my room.
4 You'd better not drive/ We'd better not go too fast.
5 We'd better do some studying.

C 1 I'm/I am supposed to take two before meals.
2 They're/They are supposed to report to the police.
3 You're/You are supposed to stand in a line.
4 They aren't supposed to watch it.

D 1 We had/We'd better hurry. OR We should hurry./ We ought to hurry.
2 We had/We'd better not be OR We ought not to be/ We shouldn't be
3 should arrive/ought to arrive
4 You shouldn't take/You ought not to take
5 We aren't supposed to get

Pages 32–33

A 1 Can I have a fork, please?
2 Could I have a towel, please?
3 Would you mind answering the phone?

B 1 must
2 have
3 like
4 want
5 Can/Could
6 Would
7 wonder
8 Can/Could

C 1 Can I have a receipt, please?/ Can you give me a receipt, please?
2 Could you tell me the time, please?
3 Can you help me, please?
4 Could I have a bag, please?/ Could you give me a bag, please?
5 Would you mind clearing a space (on the table), please?
6 Could I speak to the manager, please?

Pages 34–35

A 1 swept
2 burst
3 were rescued
4 received
5 reached
6 were blocked
7 were brought
8 is being done
9 said

B 1 my brother
2 The water
3 a driver
4 the alarm
5 The guide
6 The dog

C 1 was won by Gavin Iles.
2 went skydiving last week.
3 been attacked by a bear.
4 being built.
5 likes Marcie.
6 been thrown away.
7 been kidnapped by Martians.
8 was seen by five people.

Pages 36–37

A 1 was taken
2 was done
3 was interviewed by a very nice young police officer
4 fingerprints were found (by detectives)
5 burglar was identified (by the police database).
6 has been arrested
7 (he) is being questioned
8 jewellery hasn't been found

B 1 didn't produce many cars for sale.
2 production was started by a German called Karl Benz.
3 is now seen as the father of the automobile.

C 1 People should use them/bicycles for short trips.
2 someone has discovered a new source of energy?
3 they're/they are going to tear it down/tear down this building.
4 you shouldn't keep them/ eggs in a freezer.
5 people put it/trash in the garbage can?

Pages 38–39

A 1 to get
2 to leave
3 staying
4 sitting
5 touring
6 to go
7 to rent
8 driving
9 to spend
10 taking

B 1 taking
2 losing
3 to insist
4 arguing
5 to be
6 to repair
7 waiting
8 to have
9 to accept
10 saying

C 1 I don't mind asking to see the manager.
2 Mathieu admitted promising to go to Scotland.
3 the band happened to finish playing.

Pages 40–41

A 1 Guy invited Roxy to come on his talk show.
2 Sarah reminded Mark to get the theatre tickets.
3 The dentist told Deshawn to give up eating candy.
4 The police ordered the gunman to come out with his hands up.

B 1 don't want her to go skydiving
2 doesn't want him to fall in love with her
3 would like/'d like her to go (on vacation) with them

C 1 The police must stop the suspects leaving the country.
2 The prime minister didn't expect Parliament to oppose him.

3 The bank robbers forced the hostages to lie down.
4 The government doesn't mind the dollar falling in value.

D 1 to travel
2 buying
3 to use
4 to take

Pages 42–43

A 1 He can't think of what to say.
2 They're not sure/They aren't sure where to go.
3 She doesn't know how to stop.

B 1 what to expect
2 where to go
3 how to find
4 what to do
5 who to contact

C 1 whether to do
2 how much (money) to spend
3 whether to join
4 which route to take
5 which (lottery numbers) to choose

Pages 44–45

A 1 simple to use the computer.
2 difficult to understand the set-up.
3 It's easy to run any kind of software.
4 It's absolutely fascinating to explore the world of Compex.
5 Are you ready to try the ultimate computer experience?

B 1 is very simple to use.
2 isn't difficult to understand.
3 Any kind of software is easy to run.
4 The world of Compex is absolutely fascinating to explore.

C 1 it's/it is likely to be pretty crowded.
2 she's/she is certain to be there.
3 you're/you are unlikely to find it. OR you'll be unlikely to find it.

D 1 of
2 for
3 of
4 of
5 for

Pages 46–47

A 1 (just) can't wait for it to arrive.
2 It would be a mistake for him to marry her.
3 It's important for advertisements to tell the truth.

B 1 There's a fun pool for children to swim in.
2 There are quiet areas for you to relax in.
3 There are regular shows for you to enjoy.
4 There's a giant roller coaster for you to ride on (if you dare).

C 1 It's/It is too high for her to reach.
2 It's/It is too difficult for us to understand.
3 It wasn't loud enough for them/everyone to hear.
4 It wasn't hot enough for him to drink.

D 1 difficult for the town to attract new industry.
2 very generous of the council to give the land to Sanko.
3 is eager for production to begin soon.

Pages 48–49

A 1 have something to eat.
2 nice to take a break.
3 wants Connie to speak to him.
4 Hiroshi doesn't know how to fix the TV.
5 Ling and her sister have decided to go to Mexico.
6 Morgan has gone to the hospital to visit James.
7 (Unfortunately) Sasha has to do some studying.
8 It's important for Bida to call the office.

B 1 see/read
2 drive/go
3 cry/weep
4 lie/sit/stay
5 snow
6 see/visit

C 1 to visit
2 to see
3 to have
4 buy
5 to read
6 read
7 feel
8 look
9 get
10 to leave
11 to transfer
12 forget
13 to get

Pages 50–51

A 1 of falling
2 of dropping them
3 to move

B 1 Effem was afraid to jump.
2 Olga was afraid to argue with the policeman.
3 Maurice is afraid of getting sunburnt.

C 1 to buy
2 of getting
3 of being
4 to read
5 to reserve

D 1 about being so rude
2 about losing my temper
3 to interrupt you

Pages 52–53

A 1 I saw him take it.
2 I watched him leave (the restaurant).
3 I heard him drive away.

B 1 I can hear it ringing.
2 I can see her waving.
3 I can hear them barking.
4 I can smell it burning.

C 1 She felt the building shake.
2 He heard people shouting.
3 She could hear an alarm ringing.
4 They saw the police arrive.
5 He saw a woman crying.

Pages 54–55

A 1 is
2 are
3 look
4 are
5 has
6 costs
7 have
8 weren't

B 1 was
2 were
3 was
4 were
5 were
6 were
7 was
8 was/were

C 1 is
2 isn't
3 are
4 work
5 have
6 is
7 is
8 has

D 1 Fifteen kilometres is a long walk.
2 Eight students are travelling on the bus.
3 Three people were waiting for the museum to open.

4 Twenty kilograms is the baggage allowance.

Pages 56–57

A 1 an, the
2 The, a
3 The, an
4 an, the
5 a, the
6 the, a

B 1 a, a
2 a, a, a/the, a
3 the, a
4 the, a, an, the
5 the, a, the, the, a, The, a
6 the, a, a, the, the

C 1 a DJ
2 a VIP
3 an OPP officer
4 a PC
5 an LA suburb
6 a UFO
7 an AGM
8 an MP

Pages 58–59

A 1 some luggage
2 some flowers
3 a cat
4 some birds
5 some fruit

B 1 a
2 One
3 One
4 a

C 1 A violin is a musical instrument.
2 A kayak is a small boat.
3 An atlas is a book of maps.
4 A spade is a tool for digging.

D 1 some nuts
2 water
3 some clothes
4 delicious bread
5 (university) students

Pages 60–61

A 1 He likes fries.
2 She likes dogs.
3 He likes art.
4 She likes chemistry.

B 1 dogs, the dogs
2 cars, pollution, cars, airplanes, the pollution
3 the birds, birds, wildlife
4 history, the history, museums, old buildings

C 1 the atom
2 football
3 the guitar
4 television
5 the telescope

Pages 62–63

A 1 Thanksgiving, October
2 the weekend, Saturday
3 Christmas, a white Christmas
4 the summer, 2008
5 the afternoon, the year
6 night, the dark, the day

B 1 breakfast
2 lunch
3 the lunch
4 the dinner
5 a fantastic meal

C 1 breakfast
2 midnight
3 Christmas
4 Wednesday
5 the morning
6 night
7 the day
8 Wednesday
9 the Wednesday
10 February

Pages 64–65

A 1 the boy's bike
2 the girls' tent
3 the children's skateboards
4 the girl's cat
5 the boys' trophies

B 1 the twins'
2 Luke's
3 Jason's
4 Nicola's
5 her children's
6 the Polewskis'
7 Olivia's

C 1 Mr. Malveaux's Gun
2 The Smell of Blood
3 The Killer's Car
4 The Middle of the Night
5 The Death of Someone Important
6 The Gangsters' Money

D 1 yesterday's paper
2 five minutes' rest
3 this month's special offer
4 in a week's time

Pages 66–67

A 1 's/is looking at herself (in the mirror).
2 're/are introducing themselves.
3 He's/He is teaching himself Arabic.
4 She's/She is drying herself (with a towel).

B 1 yourself
2 ourselves
3 itself

C 1 you
2 him
3 himself
4 her
5 yourself

D 1 feel
2 help yourselves
3 remember
4 worry
5 relax

Pages 68–69

A 1 everyone/everybody, no one/nobody
2 someone/somebody, something
3 somewhere, Someone/somebody
4 everywhere, nothing

B 1 someone
2 anyone
3 somewhere
4 anywhere
5 anything
6 something

C 1 his
2 it
3 likes, they
4 has, their

D 1 I once met someone famous.
2 Someone's car is blocking me in.
3 I've got something else/something different to tell you.
4 We know everyone's opinions/opinion.
5 Everyone else except you is going.
6 Nothing exciting ever happens here.

Pages 70–71

A 1 exhausted
2 interested
3 fascinating
4 exciting

B 1 surprised
2 disappointing
3 confusing
4 bored
5 interesting

C 1 relaxing
2 annoyed
3 amused
4 interested
5 fascinating
6 thrilling
7 exhausting

Pages 72–73

A
1 brightly
2 patiently
3 immediately
4 punctually
5 secretly
6 safely
7 fluently
8 carefully
9 quietly

B
1 angrily
2 happily
3 automatically
4 publicly
5 enthusiastically
6 reasonably
7 securely

C
1 The Flames won the game easily.
2 I've/I have checked the figures carefully.
3 Your dog barked at me very fiercely.
4 It's/It is snowing very heavily (here).

D
1 dark
2 terribly
3 badly
4 suddenly
5 quietly
6 unhappy
7 sadly
8 curious
9 foolishly

Pages 74–77

A
1 outside
2 Perhaps
3 always
4 Obviously
5 silently
6 hard

B
1 mid
2 end
3 front
4 mid
5 mid
6 mid
7 end
8 front
9 mid
10 mid

C
1 clearly crossed
2 will probably rain
3 didn't fully understand
4 are usually
5 occasionally visited it/visited it occasionally
6 were immediately working
7 has obviously forgotten

D
1 It usually rains when Stanley is on vacation.
2 Natalia's friend visits her most weekends.
3 Eric gets a pay raise every year.
4 Christine never checks her work.

E
1 I've always known your secret.
2 We certainly can't afford a new car. OR Certainly we can't afford a new car.
3 The tourists didn't walk far.
4 Jevani cut the paper carefully./ Jevani carefully cut the paper.
5 Olivia can also play the violin. OR Olivia can play the violin also.
6 I read the newspaper most days./ Most days I read the newspaper.

F
1 peacefully at his home
2 through the streets yesterday
3 to Mexico last year
4 there in June

G
1 We had a lovely time in the country.
2 We arrived home safely at about eight.
3 You should come and visit us soon. OR You should come soon and visit us.
4 It's always nice to see you and Tony.
5 Maybe you'll be able to come in the New Year./You'll be able to come in the New Year, maybe. OR You'll maybe be able to come in the New Year.
6 We'll see you sometime.

Pages 78–81

A
1 up
2 in/inside
3 above/over
4 down
5 by/beside/next to
6 around/by
7 in front of
8 away from/out of

B
1 behind, through, below
2 past, down, opposite

C
1 opposite
2 between
3 opposite
4 between
5 next to

D
1 under
2 up
3 on
4 around
5 into
6 out of

E
1 to
2 outside
3 into
4 past/by
5 off
6 on
7 through
8 near
9 among

Pages 82–83

A
1 since
2 for
3 since
4 for

B
1 He's/He has been in bed for three days.
2 They've/They have been in the backyard since breakfast.
3 He's/He has been at his desk since nine o'clock.
4 She's/She has been on the road for five hours.

C
1 since four o'clock
2 ten years ago
3 since Monday/since then
4 for six weeks
5 for three years
6 eight months ago
7 for three weeks

D
1 earlier
2 ago
3 earlier

Pages 84–85

A
1 into
2 from
3 as
4 with/to
5 to
6 to
7 with

B
1 prefer water to wine?
2 blaming Tom for the/his accident?
3 thank you for the/her present?
4 accuse him/the history professor of murder?
5 provide you with towels? OR provide towels for you?
6 invite you to her wedding?
7 congratulate them on the/their (great) victory?
8 pointed a gun at Melanie?

C
1 about
2 of
3 to
4 to
5 about/of
6 about
7 about/of

Pages 86–87

A
1 stay in
2 pay … back
3 fall over
4 lie down
5 cut out
6 come back
7 get on
8 take … back
9 go away
10 give away

B
1 left out
2 sent out/handed out
3 throw away/throw out
4 put off
5 made up
6 go on/carry on/keep on

C
1 picks … up
2 put on/put … on
3 find … out
4 hand in/hand … in
5 written … down
6 win back
7 put away/put … away
8 look … up
9 held up
10 mixing … up

Pages 88–89

A
1 John
2 2010
3 April
4 (about) two weeks

B
1 you
2 he, your
3 he, you

C
1 the day before
2 that day
3 here
4 the week before

Pages 90–91

A
1 was
2 was
3 is OR was
4 was
5 was OR is

B
1 you had finished it/your project.
2 you weren't on a diet.
3 you didn't enjoy them/parties.
4 you weren't applying for it/ the job.

C
1 *The Times* said the production was amazing.
2 Steve Devine said he couldn't remember a funnier show.
3 Sharida Birani said it (had) made her laugh.
4 *The Canadian Globe* said you/ people had to see it. OR *The Canadian Globe* said you/ people must see it.
5 *The City Star* said it would be a great success.
6 *The Express* said you/people might die laughing.
7 Marcel Chauvin said it was the funniest show he'd/he had ever seen.
8 *Entertainment Monthly* said you/people shouldn't miss it.

Pages 92–93

A
1 She wants to know how she can find out about the area.
2 He wants to know if/whether there are any guided tours.
3 They want to know where they can stay.
4 They want to know what shows there are.

B
1 Do you know if I can park here?
2 Could you tell me how long the movie lasts?
3 Do you know how often the buses run?
4 Do you know if we are/ we're allowed to smoke?
5 Could you tell me what time the flight is?
6 Could you tell me how much a ticket costs?

C
1 why I wanted the job.
2 how I (had) heard about it.
3 if/whether I was hard-working.
4 if/whether I could work on Saturdays.
5 how I would/I'd travel to work.
6 if/whether I had a bicycle.
7 how much I hoped to earn.
8 when I could start.

Pages 94–95

A
1 The doctor told him to get more exercise.
2 His boss asked/told him not to play computer games at the office.
3 A police officer told him (that) he couldn't park his car on Queen Street.
4 Shanti asked him to hang some pictures up.

B
1 Craig to take a break.
2 for forgetting to get groceries.
3 singing a few songs.
4 Fone-Ning to mail a/the letter.
5 making a mistake.
6 Sam not to touch the wires.

C
1 The builders have promised that everything will be ready on time.
2 The boss insists that we (have to) check the figures carefully.
3 Warren has admitted that his story wasn't completely true.
4 Gino reminded Bella that her train was about to leave.

Pages 96–97

A
1 the young man at the door
2 the man who plays his stereo at night
3 the very thin woman
4 the girl with green eyes (or the green-eyed girl)
5 the young woman in the office
6 the man who drives a taxi
7 the smart young man
8 the student who failed all her exams

B
1 that/which
2 who/that
3 who/that
4 that/which
5 that/which
6 who/that

C
1 The earthquake which occurred in Chile caused a lot of damage.
2 The scientist who discovered a new planet has won the Nobel Prize.
3 The hockey player who injured his opponent has been suspended for ten games.
4 The little girl who had been missing since Thursday has been found safe and well.
5 The company which owns Car-Co Manufacturing has laid off thousands of employees.
6 The 75-year-old woman who went bungee jumping now wants to swim across Lake Ontario.

Pages 98–99

A
1 Felix Reeves is the journalist whose tape recorder was stolen.
2 Graham Wilshaw is the architect who knew Maurice in school.
3 Frank Lafferty is the farmer whose land Maurice bought.
4 Sal Politano is the lawyer who looked after Maurice's interests.
5 Sonia Goldman is the house guest whose fingerprints were on the doorknob.

B 1 What you have to think about is your profit.
2 What you must know are the needs of your customers.
3 What you should work towards is a realistic target.
4 What you need to do is (to) plan ahead.

C 1 Cartier sailed to Canada.
2 soccer that Chelsea Stewart plays.
3 It was in Greece that the Olympic Games first took place.
4 It's/It is Mercury that is closest to the sun.

Pages 100–1

A 1 If the twins had worn different clothes, we could have told them apart. Third
2 If you tell me what the instructions say, I'll try to follow them. First
3 If people used public transportation, there'd be less pollution. Second
4 If you don't wear a sweater, you might not be warm enough. First
5 If I hadn't seen the product advertised, I wouldn't have bought it. Third

B 1 you played
2 I wouldn't/couldn't hear
3 you'd/you had told
4 I wouldn't have rented
5 you didn't play
6 it wouldn't be/it might not be
7 I'd/I had realized
8 I would have thrown
9 you go on
10 I'll have

C 1 If I'd/I had known how unpopular Jason was, I wouldn't have invited him (to my party).
2 If you put too many cans into the plastic bag, it'll break.
3 If I had a pen, I could write down the address.
4 If I'd/I had started my project earlier, I wouldn't be so far behind (now).
5 If you need some/any help, call me.
6 If the door opens, the fan comes on.

Pages 102–3

A 1 but it's actually very modern.
2 but she turned it down.
3 but no one laughed.

B 1 Although
2 in spite of
3 Although
4 in spite of
5 in spite of

C 1 in spite of/despite
2 In spite of/Despite
3 but/although/though
4 Even though/Although/ Though

D 1 Ethan didn't notice the sign even though it was right in front of him.
2 Richard doesn't know any French although he studied it in high school.
3 Despite being a millionaire, Henri's friend hates spending money.
4 We couldn't get tickets in spite of lining up for an hour.

E 1 on the other hand
2 in spite of/despite
3 whereas

Pages 104–5

A 1 to go to sleep.
2 to hear the local news.
3 to look professional.
4 to pay her tuition.

B 1 He's/He is going to get to work earlier in order to/so as to impress the boss.
2 He's/He is going to work harder in order to/so as to achieve more.
3 He's/He is going to take risks in order to/so as to be a winner.
4 He's/He is going to think positively in order not to/so as not to miss any opportunities.

C 1 Tanya keeps a dog to guard the house.
2 David is going to be very careful so that he doesn't/ won't have an accident.
3 Jessica is going on a diet to lose weight.
4 Marisol often turns off the heat to save money.
5 Talia had to go to Montreal for a business meeting.
6 Isabel wore boots so that her feet wouldn't get cold.

Pages 106–9

The number after each answer indicates the page number on which you can find information about that grammar point.

1 c 2
2 d 2
3 c 4
4 d 6
5 b 8
6 d 10
7 b 12
8 d 14
9 b 16
10 a 20
11 c 22
12 b 24
13 d 26
14 b 28
15 c 30
16 b 34, 36
17 d 38
18 b 38
19 b or c 40
20 d 42
21 b 46
22 d 52
23 d 56
24 a 60
25 a 66
26 c 68
27 a 72
28 b 74
29 c 78
30 c 82
31 d 84
32 d 86
33 a 88
34 c 90
35 d 94
36 d 96
37 c 98
38 a 100
39 b 100
40 d 100
41 d 102
42 d 104

Index